The Power Within a Poem

****

A Passionately Fair Publisher

Self edited by each Author / Poet
Manuscript formatting, cover designing,
Interior artwork designed
By
Pat Simpson
www.apfpublisher.com

ISBN: 978-1-329-40380-2

Foreword

A “P.F.P” Poem
Is a poem created from another poem!
Here within this books pages you will find
Some great P.F.P. poems written by many of todays
Most accomplished and published Poets.
Poems that have been composed
From a weekly challenge poem
Set by the Challenge Master Poet Erich J. Goller.
"To compete in the challenge poets must
Pick out 20 words maximum
From the set weekly poem to create another poem,
Entire phrases from the poem must never be used
It can be written in any style with or without rhyme
And it must have a different title,
Now please settle back and enjoy reading all
The included accomplishments portrayed here
Within the pages of this with
“Thanks! To All Participating Poets“
Our seventh book in series

****

Contents

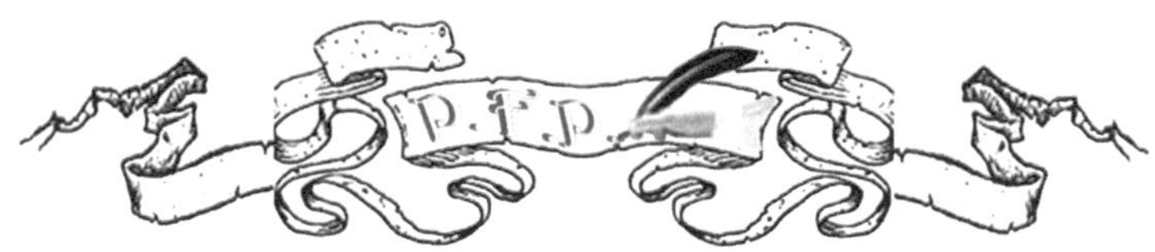

Contents

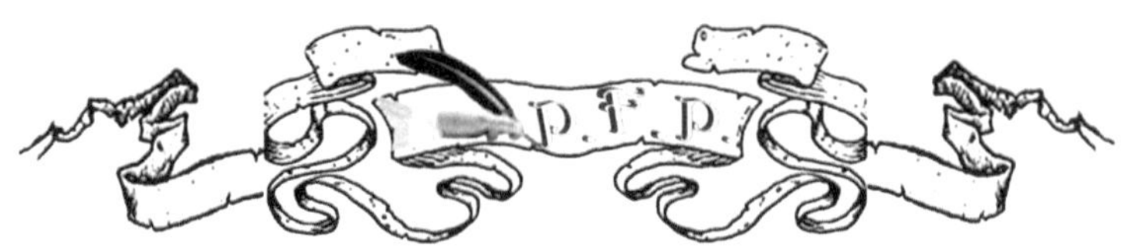

Contents

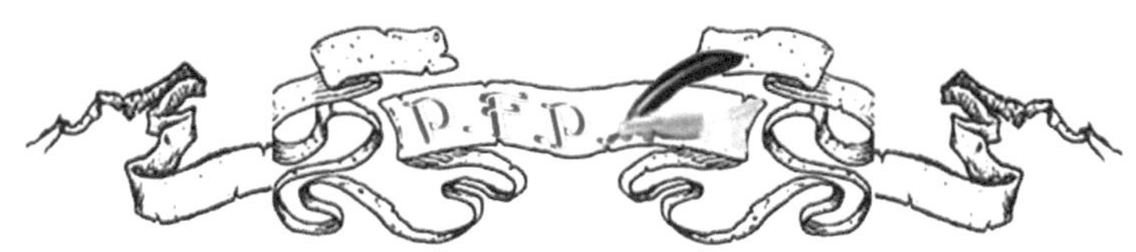

Contents

Contents

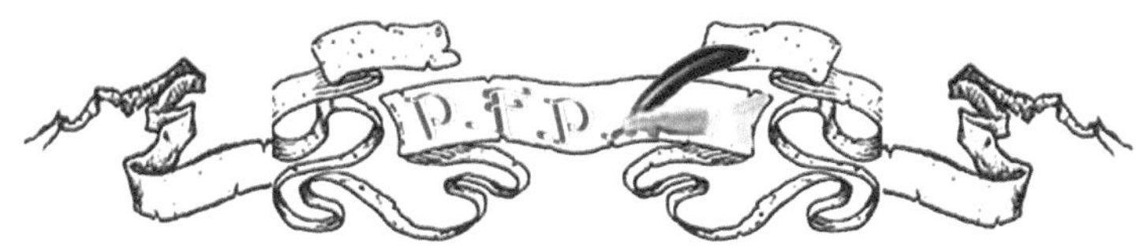

Contents

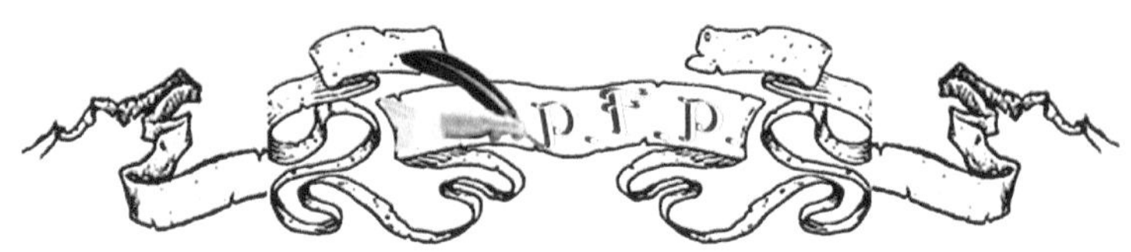

Contents

****

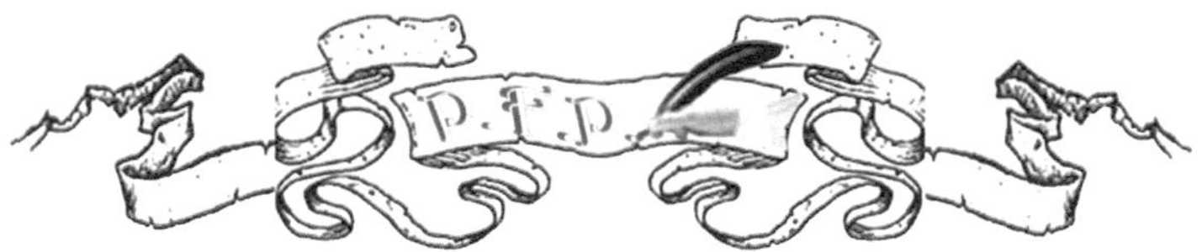

Erich J. Goller

Alliance Challenge Master

Erich J. Goller

The Writers And Poetry Alliance

Bard

The Writers & Poetry Alliance
Presents This Certificate
To Poet
Erich J. Goller
For Excellent Achievement
In All Styled Poetry!

STYLIST

Vienna

http://apfpublisher.com/Erich.html
http://www.poetvienna.com/

****

Beautiful Arrayed

(Starter Poem 1)

The wintry north extend their blast
Leafless trees, freezing winter days
Sweeping winds, the sky is overcast
Each season has their charming ways

There's the harvest moon at night
In nature's spectacular show
It is beauty of pure delight
Everywhere you look and go

With blending songs of earth and sky
Wildflowers gracing the landscape
Way up pillow clouds sailing by
Mountain tops, shaded woodland glade

Somewhere above a distant land
The nights are dark and there's no moon
Where many different colors blend
The stars do brighten up the gloom

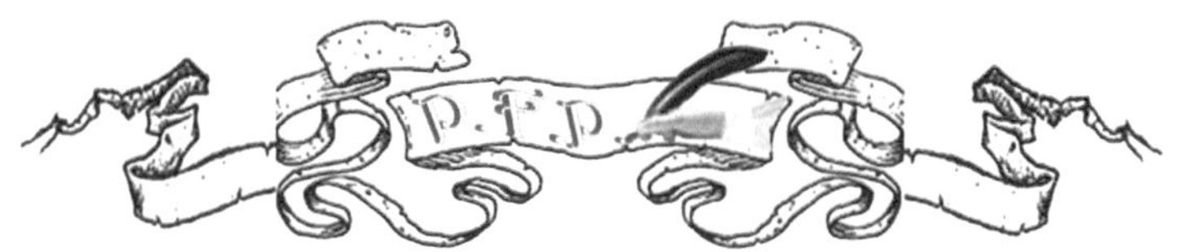

Every thing that's bright and fair
It is all beautiful arrayed
Earth blessed with heavenly air
These treasure the Master has made.

© Erich J. Goller

****

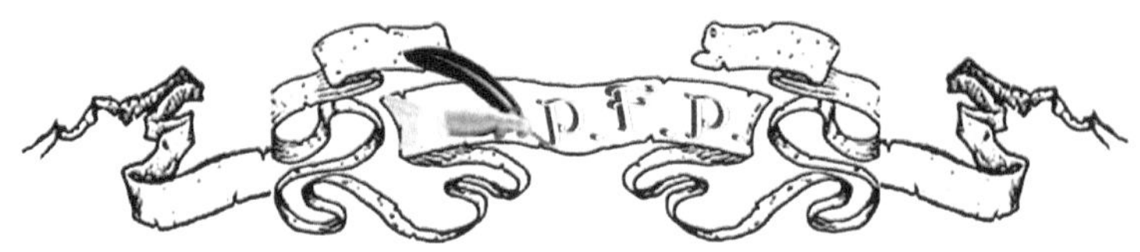

Sweeping Colors

Sweeping Colors brighten
the spectacular moon gloom,
gracing the fluffy pillow clouded sky
and the earth the Master has blessed.

© Erich J. Goller

****

Nature's Song

In a distant mountain
Trees and wildflowers
Sweeping the landscapes
With charming beauty
Nature blessed each of you
with song

© Dena M. Ferrari

****

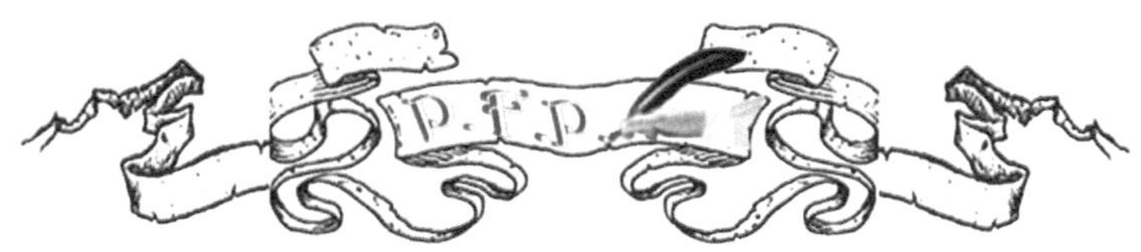

Heavenly Blessed

Heavenly blessed is nature
Wildflowers landscape, mountain tops
Master made beauty everywhere
Treasure delight of earth and sky blending!

© Christina R Jussaume

****

Treasures To Behold

Blending of sky,
Clouds,
Heavenly pillow,
Overcast.
Moon.
Nights so dark,
Stars bright
A show spectacular.
Treasure by the Master.

© Sue White

****

senyru

heavenly treasure

sweeping beauty blending days

Master gracing stars

© Janet L. Vick

****

Pure Delight

The moon, and stars
Are pure delight
The Earth is blessed
The sky is bright

© Peter Duggan

****

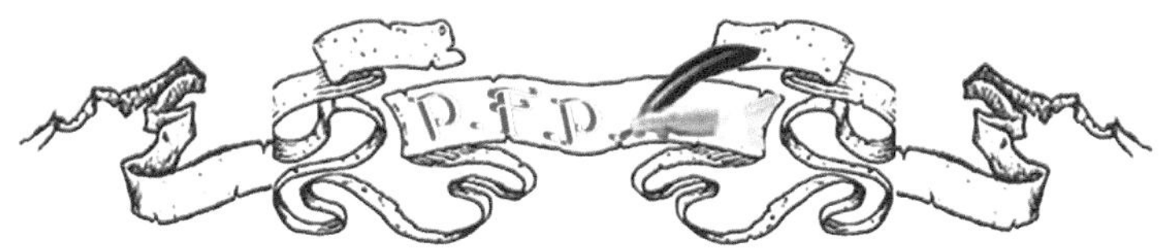

Seasons

winds
sweeping
with earth's songs…
the Master's days
blend

© Karen O'Leary

****

Heavenly Treasure

You are a heavenly treasure;
charming ways brighten
overcast days.

Spectacular beauty,
a blessed delight
the lord has made.

© Kevin Bates

****

Colorful Overflow

(Starter Poem 2)

Northern winds whisper to the trees
The shining dawn and sunset's glow
Leaves falling with the faintest breeze
Autumn's colorful overflow

With flaming hills and amber fields
From all the seasons of the year
Blessed bounty the harvest yields
Autumn is full with warmth and cheer

With color changing in the sky
Soon birds will sing their farewell song
It's time for fresh-baked pumpkin pie
Days will be short, darkness be long

Days will be short, darkness be long
It's time for fresh-baked pumpkin pie
Soon birds will sing their farewell song
With color changing in the sky

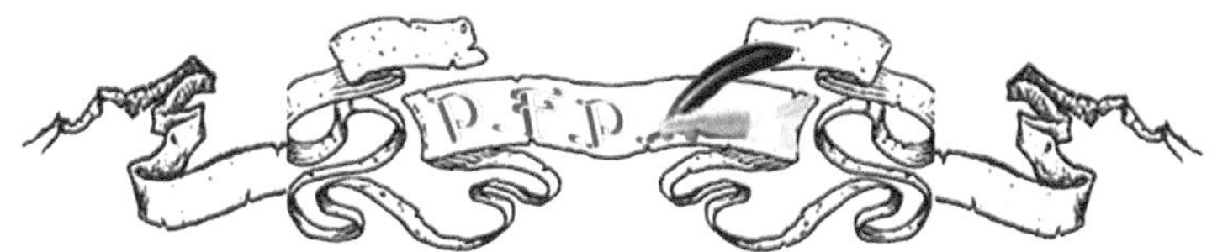

Autumn is full with warmth and cheer
Blessed bounty the harvest yields
From all the seasons of the year
With flaming hills and amber fields

Autumn's colorful overflow
Leaves falling with the faintest breeze
The shining dawn and sunset's glow
Northern winds whisper to the trees.

© Erich J. Goller

****

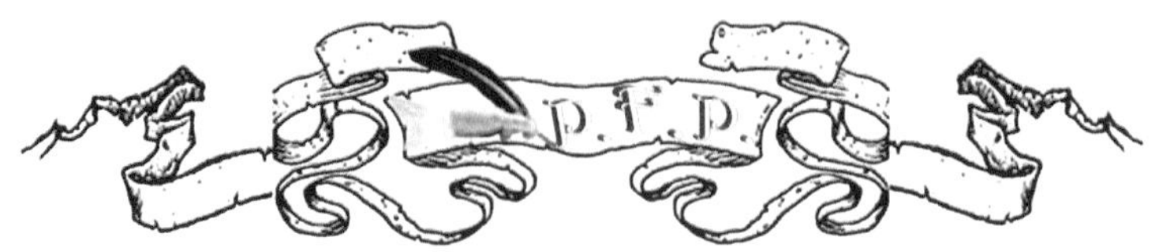

Farewell Song

Flaming Autumn season,
colorful leaves falling with cheer,
winds whisper in the trees,
the birds sing their farewell song.

© Erich J. Goller

****

The Dawn of Autumn

With the dawn of autumn
Birds sing in trees of sunsets glow
Of seasons faintest breeze
And leaves colourful overflow

© Patricia Ann Farnsworth-Simpson

****

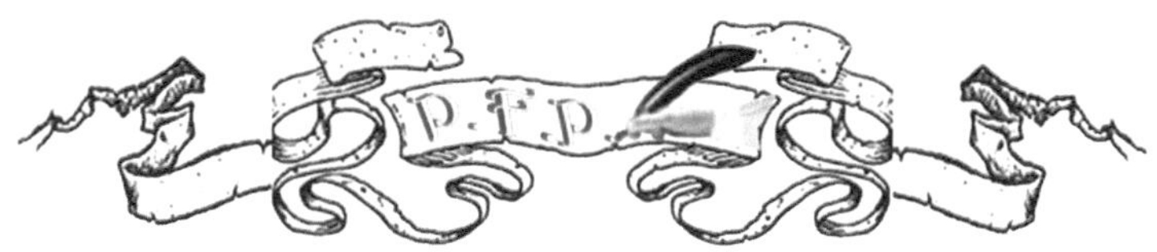

Time to Harvest

The faintest whisper of
Northern breeze
Farewell the birds
Time to harvest
The fields

© Dena M. Ferrari

****

Time to Yield

Autumn's winds whisper
Leaves falling
In the faintest breeze
Sky changing colour
Birds sing their farewell song
Time to yield

© George L. Ellison

****

Autumn Sunset

breeze
of change…
amber leaves
whisper farewell
songs

© Karen O'Leary

****

Full of Cheer

Flaming color
Autumn leaves
Sunset's breeze
Fields of bounty
Overflow of harvest
Full of cheer

© Dena M. Ferrari

****

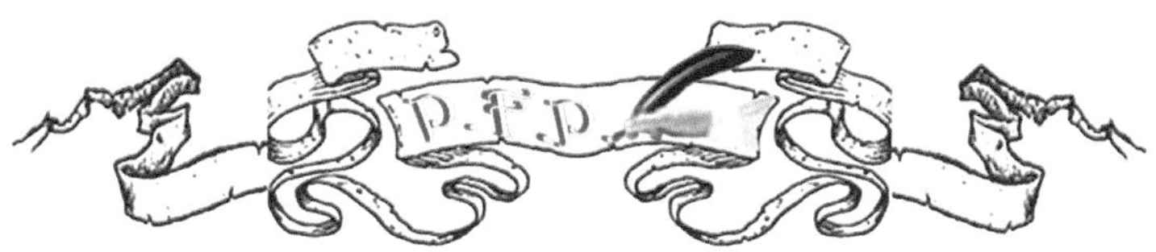

Haiku

trees whisper seasons
harvest blessed with autumn cheer
sunset's overflow

dawn shining bounty
sky yields changing amber fields
it's darkness farewell

© Janet L. Vick

****

Full of Cheer

Hills flaming with autumn cheer
It's a blessed season of the year
Full of bounty
Full of cheer

© Patricia Ann Farnsworth-Simpson

****

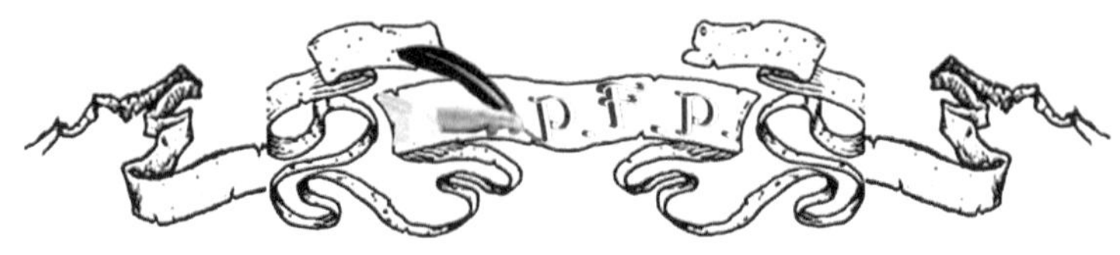

Farewell

Amber trees, the flaming sky
Winds yield, the darkness long
Leaves falling, the hills changing
Farewell is the faintest song

© John W. Henson

****

Autumn's Flaming Hills

Autumns flaming hills
Blessed bounty of harvest
Short days, darkness long
Birds sing farewell song
Northern winds with leaves falling

© Christina R Jussaume

****

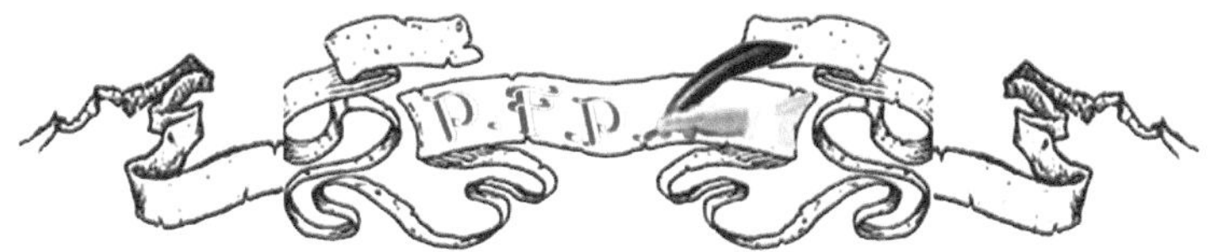

Christina R. Jussaume

Alliance Style Tutor

www.poetesscrjussaume.com

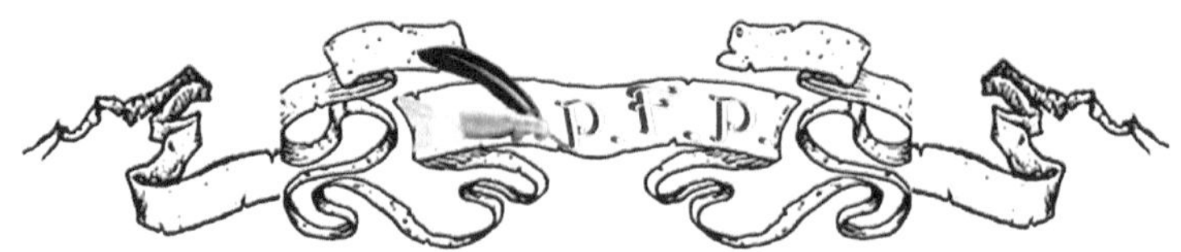

Expect Dreams Reality

(Starter Poem 3)

Always believe dreams will happen
He puts you on path to succeed
It's Lord's timetable and pattern
He is sincere and won't mislead
Each dream He has put in your heart
Feel His essence from day's start

He puts you on path to succeed
He is sincere and won't mislead

You will see your life taking shape
Stay in faith for your time's coming
Lord molds pieces and does reshape
Always believe of forthcoming
Your dreams become blessings when time
You hear angelic choir with rhyme

Stay in faith for your time's coming
Always believe of forthcoming

Obey His words in Holy book
Your hope you will then find strengthen
Feel peace as sit by babbling brook
Life you will feel has redemption
I trust Lord my dreams I will see
Forever enjoy evergreen tree

Your hope you will then find strengthen
Life you will feel has redemption

****

Believe in Dreams

His peace and essence feel,

In faith believe forthcoming

In heart dreams time coming,

On path Lord's timetable taking shape

© Christina R Jussaume

****

Forthcoming Timetable

Forthcoming timetable pattern

strengthen and reshape holy hope

to trust dreams forever to succeed

and believe in the Lord forever.

© Erich J. Goller

****

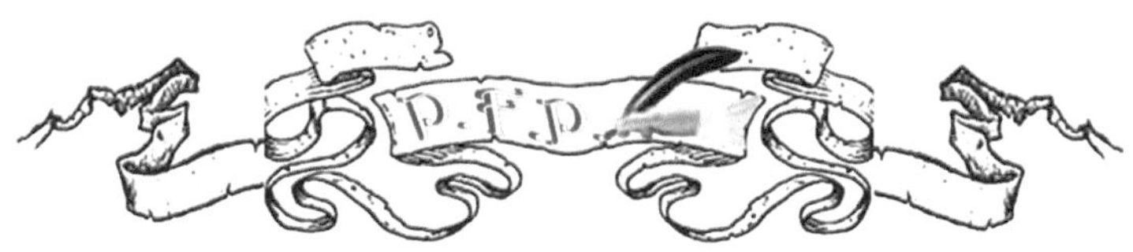

Stay in Faith

Dreams the timetable
in your sincere heart
faith molds blessings
is rhyme of your life
time always strengthen
angelic dreams

© Rhoda Galgiani

****

My Book

My book always
Becomes blessings
Words babbling
In sincere pattern
I reshape and mold my heart

~

© Dena M. Ferrari

****

Words of Faith

Find life in your book of Days

His word won't mislead

Strengthen your dreams always

Words of faith will succeed

© John W. Henson

****

Find Faith

Believe in your dreams
Of peace,
Your time it's coming
Stay sincere
And always find
Faith

© Peter Duggan

****

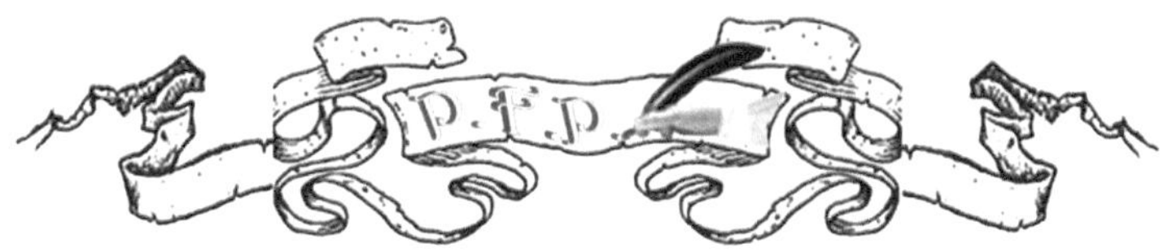

Time's Pattern

Time's pattern
forthcoming,
blessings shape
life timetable,
dreams strengthen
with sincere faith
and trust in Lord's redemption.

© Janet Vick

****

The Timetable

The pattern of life
Is the path of life
Timetable, by the lord
Succeed in life
Follow the Lord's way.

© Sue White

****

Mold and Reshape

Your dreams will
mold and reshape you
Your faith will strengthen
your heart
Your life
It's blessing

****

You Will Succeed

Time's pieces stay in dreams
You sit forever by your path
You will succeed
You won't hear
your heart mislead

****

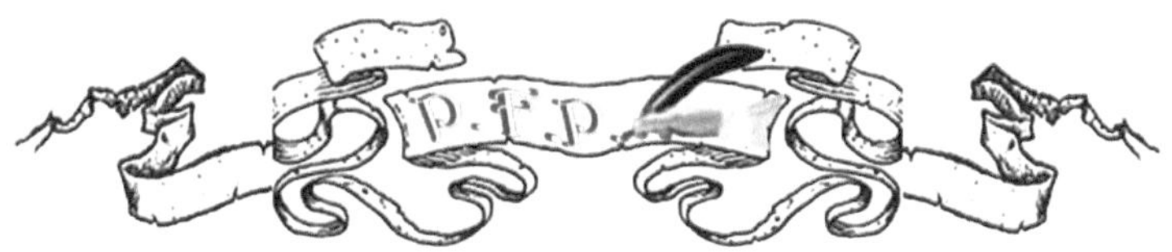

Believe in Lord

Always believe in the Lord
His words will then
You strengthen
You will succeed
Feel peace
Of forthcoming
Redemption

© Patricia Ann Farnsworth-Simpson

****

Expect Dreams Realty

Sincere dreams happen,
Believe Lord's timetable
In faith life shape,
Forever feel peace as
Blessings forthcoming,
Trust redemption will see

© Christina R. Jussaume

****

Blessed are Forgiven

(Starter Poem 4)

With an open heart do learn to change ways

Once this happens happiness fills your days

You will feel great; you will feel great!

With Bible's keys the Lord's blessing you'll find

You must be of good character and kind

You will sow seed; you will sow seed

We must also forgive those that hurt us

This is something that is really a must

You will find key; you will find key

The past slate will be wiped clean from then on

Heart will feel lighter as resentment gone

Joy felt in core; joy felt in core!

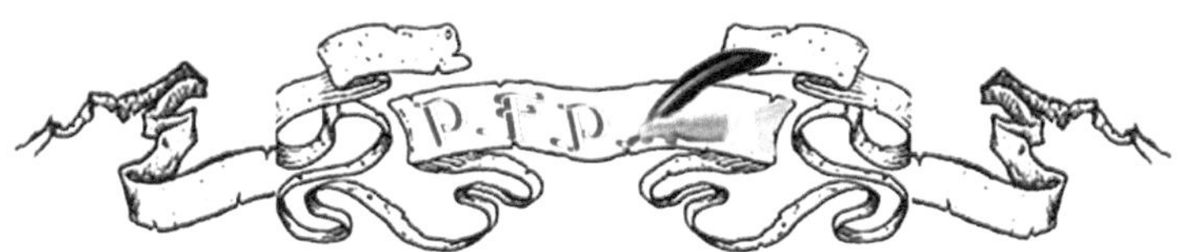

Walk in the Light of Christ forevermore

When times right you will see Heavenly door

Sing with angels; sing with angels!

****

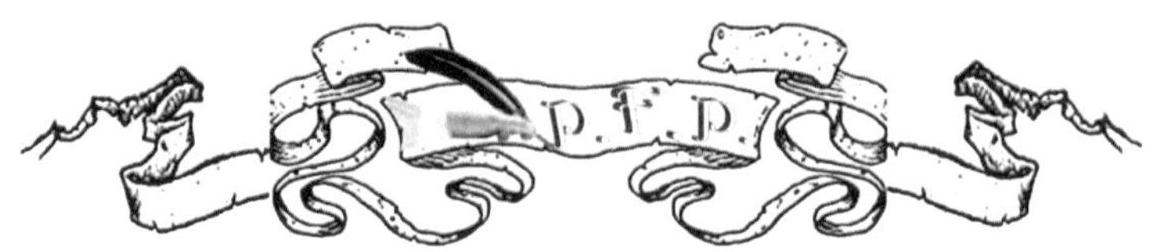

Walk in the Light

The Bible's keys change ways
Forgive hurt, slate wiped clean
Forevermore walk in the Light
With angels sing from core

© Christina R Jussaume

****

Heavenly Door

With resentment gone
happiness will feel the
great blessing and see
the light in the heavenly
door when angels sing.

© Erich J. Goller

****

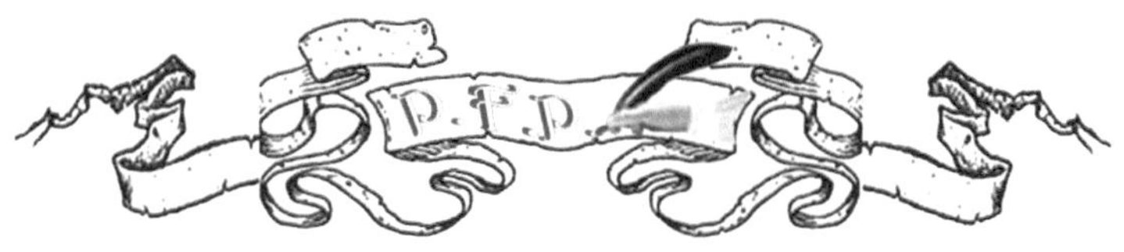

Heavenly Door

sow seeds

find keys

© Karen O 'Leary

****

Happiness is Key

Be the kind of character
You'll find
in your core
Walk past resentment
Happiness is key

© Dena M. Ferrari

****

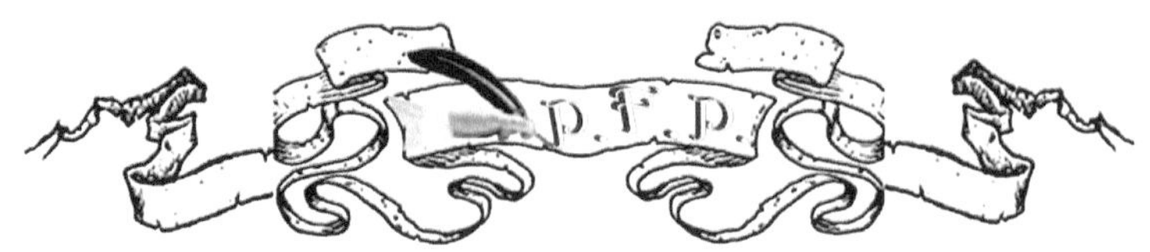

Blessings of Christ

With Angels
You will sing
With light heart forevermore
The blessings of Christ
You will find
Right in Heaven's door

© Patricia Ann Farnsworth-Simpson

****

Light of Heart

Be light of heart
Sow the seed of happiness
Forgive the past
Blessing of great joy

© Dena M. Ferrari

****

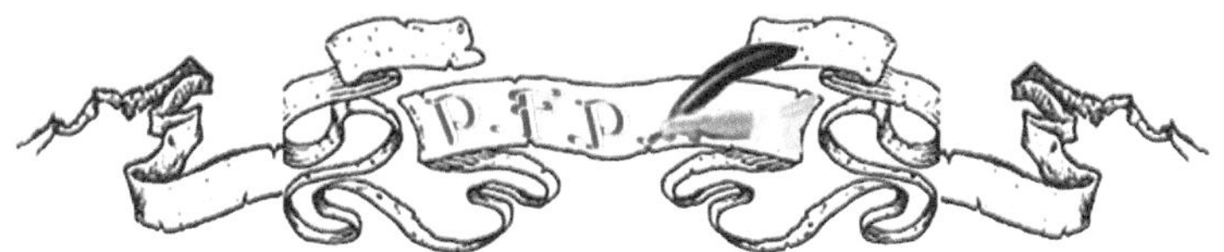

Dena M. Ferrari

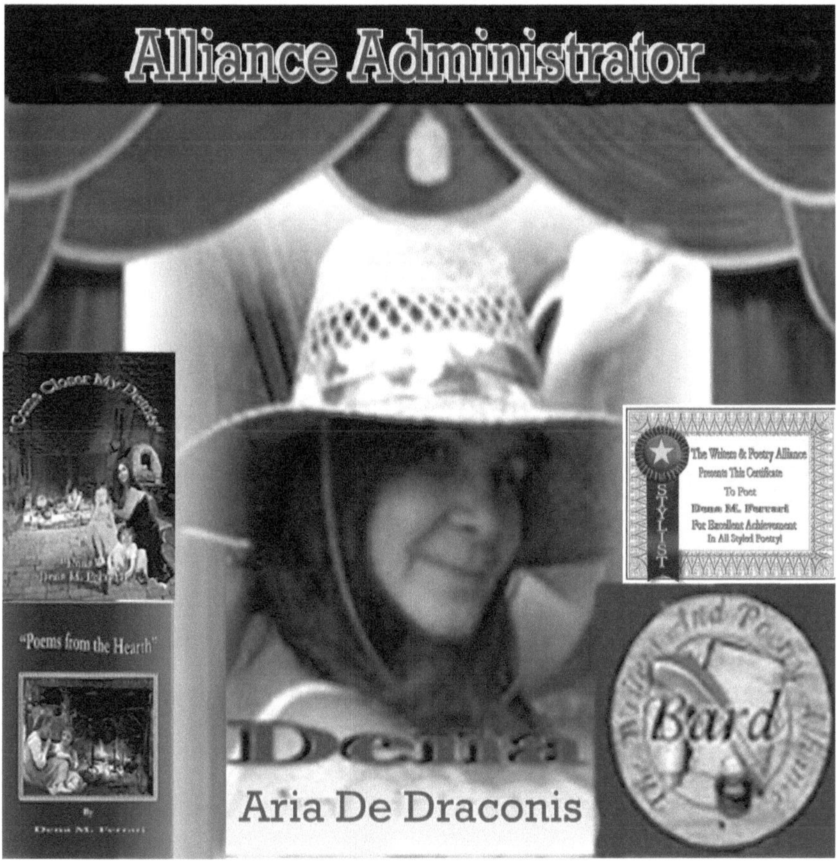

http://apfpublisher.com/Ferrari.html

****

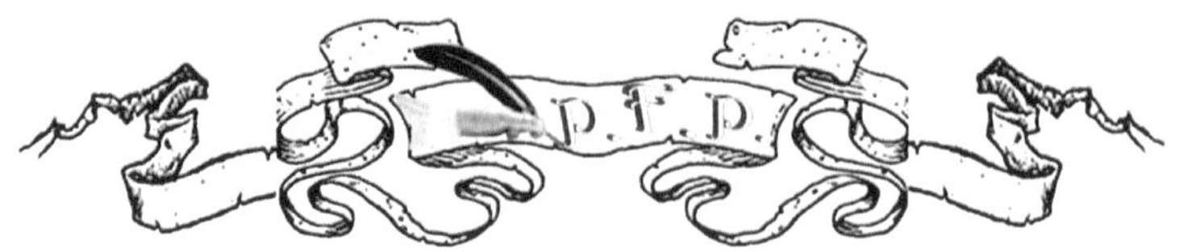

Samhaine

(Starter Poem 5)

The mirrored season at last arrives
Creeping from shadows where all Ancestors reside
Veils are the thinnest or so it seems
We call this time Samhaine...some call it Halloween.
Our New Year's Magick is about to begin
Through the night it's safe under our skin
A twinkling of the eye plus a wish come true
We all grow wiser before the Cycle of the Wheel is through.

Harvest is reaped from what spring had been sown
Death comes so that new life can be grown
A time of endings and of beginnings
All of nature enjoys the autumns winnings
Colors of red yellow green brown and gold
It has been the cycle from our Ancestors of old.
Ancient oak bows her branches dance and sway
Enjoying the attention as Death brings decay.

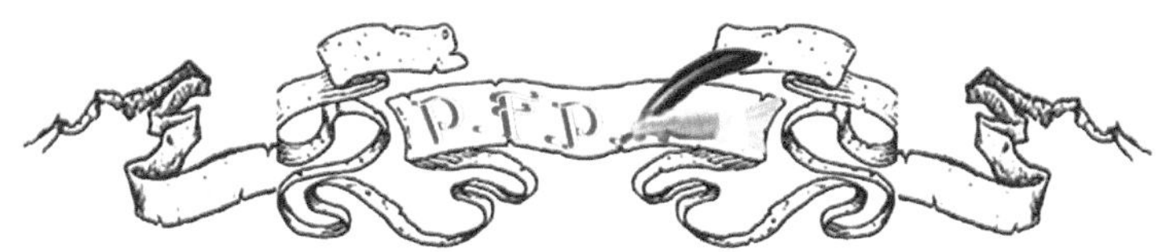

Life in this season begins its long sleep
Winter fast approaches so slumber must be deep.
Before that time comes to pass
Fall brings a crispness that defies summers heated blast.
Seek the Mirror that shows your fate
Throw away the sorrows fury hurts and hate
A Blessing upon those when wisdom has shown
The way to go forward on your journey back home.

© Dena M. Ferrari

****

Veils Sway

A new beginning
From where we sleep
Our magick night begun
Twinkling veils sway
Defies death that arrives
in slumber

© Dena M. Ferrari

****

Our Last Season

Reaped and sown
Beginnings and endings
Life and death
Bows
At our last season
We dance
before we decay

© Dena M. Ferrari

****

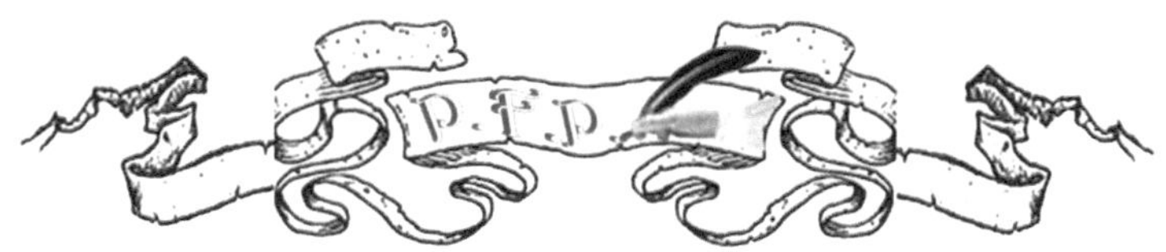

Harvest

Natures heated summers
dance is enjoying the
blessing and attention of
the seasons life's harvest
twinkling red, gold and yellow

© Erich J. Goller

****

The Season Arrives

Autumn's about
The season arrives
Nature is in sleep
A sleep so deep
That nature enjoys

© Peter Duggan

****

Beginnings

season
of spring shadows--
the dance of oak branches
that decay in autumn's journey
…endings

© Karen O'Leary

****

Magick Slumber

As shadows of the night

Comes creeping in

A magick slumber fast approaches

For a long sleep journey to begin

© Patricia Ann Farnsworth-Simpson

****

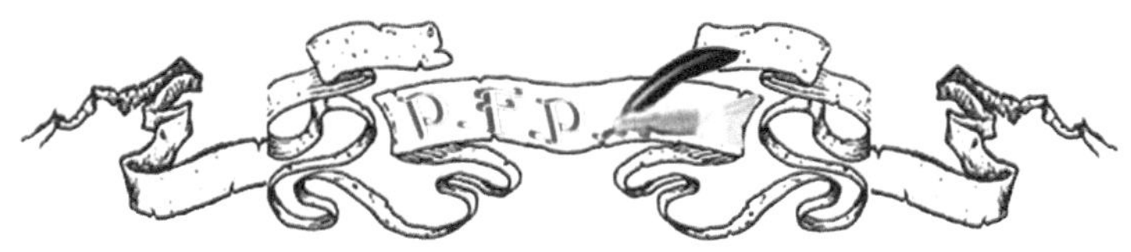

Fate or Magick

Thinnest veils dance over skin,
A twinkling eye,
Her dance, her sway
Magick sown
Brings heated attention
Through the night.

© Sue White

****

The Cycle

Life season begins
winter brings a long sleep
time of endings, to go forward
to your journey cycle back home

© Rhoda Galgiani

****

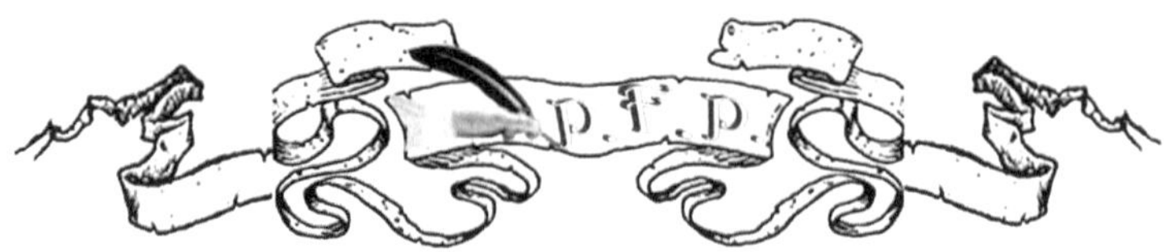

Bard of the Wood

(Starter Poem 6)

I bid thee welcome weary traveler
Soon you'll be to the place you're after
I am but a humble Bard of the Wood
Pull close your mantle and warm hood

Chanced you did the fears of the forest's most cruel
By my fire please sit share a bowl of meager gruel
Daylight sleeps calmly chasing feared thoughts away
Night time is upon you in these woods won't you stay?

Never fret at the howl of the lone wolf
By my fire he'll sit as friendship's proof
Show no fear as he settles and curls
He too awaits a story to unfurl

The beast curled beside you feels your pain
Looks like you both will have something good to gain
Your hand strokes the thickened fur without thought
Trust is now a well worn commodity that can't be bought

So where do we start on this fine chilled eve
What wonders to experience and believe
Ah yes I can see it now in your tired eyes
So much sorrow has poured from dark skies

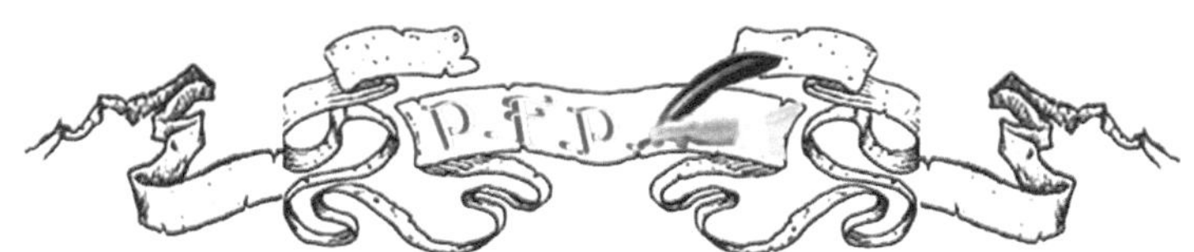

A restless wind blows from the northeast
Chills the bones with a blast of winters feast
The fires flicker when the new log is laid
Shooting sparks high as they glitter and fade

So the Bard the traveler and the wolf passed the time
Listening to a new tale of a knight who's fame did climb
The fire flickered and crackled with time well spent
Smoke tendrils upward as the story's blessings are sent

****

New Experience

A humble blessing to you
Friendship's share a thought
Never show restless fear
Welcome calmly
the new experience

© Dena M. Ferrari

****

Dark Skies

Listening to the lone wolf
howl in the wood as the
restless chilled nighttime wind
blows throughout northwest
dark skies.

© Erich J. Goller

****

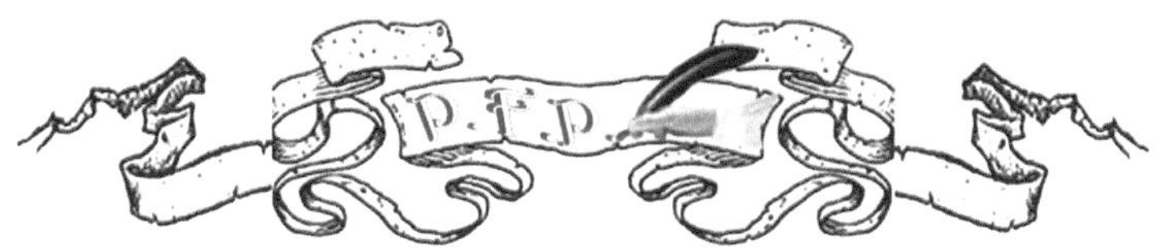

The Wind Blows

humble
trust worn weary…
the chilled lone traveler
warms when a flicker of friendship
unfurls

© Karen O'Leary

****

Sleep now

Your tired eyes sleep now
As the fires flicker
And sparks glitter
In a night time
Of no fear

© Peter Duggan

****

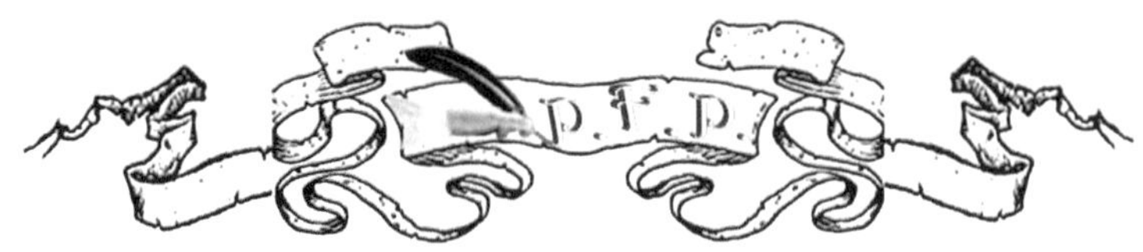

Can't Stay

I sit calmly by the fire
Weary I pull my mantle close
This chilled to the bones nighttime
Can't stay

© Dena M. Ferrari

****

Hypnotic Trust

Curled by the fire
Trust of humble Bard
Calmly settles
A weary traveller's
Restless tired eyes
As story's tendrils unfurl

© George L. Ellison

****

The Traveler

Sorrow sparks,
settles in fears
thickened pain...
Weary tendrils
dark flicker
curled, restless beast,
the traveler without trust.

© Janet L.Vick

****

Fire Sparks

Fire sparks the woods
Chased by restless wind sent
Shooting strokes most cruel
Smoke thickened with time spent

© Patricia Ann Farnsworth-Simpson

****

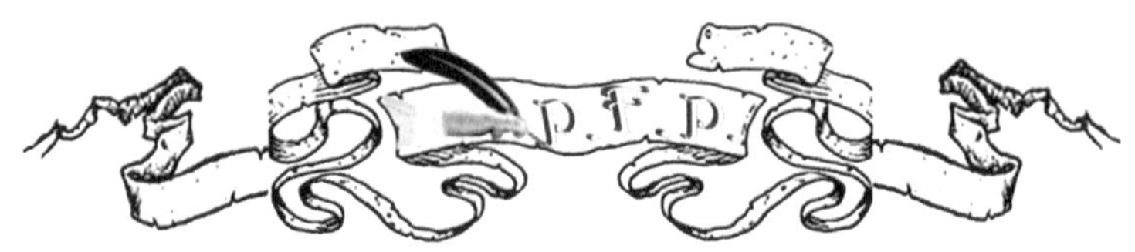

The Commodity of Trust

Traveler and wolf share fire
Hand strokes beast's fur
Experience trust listening to tale
Story's blessings unfurl
In friendship proof

© Christina R Jussaume

****

The Howl

A fur mantle, winter's chills
Fires flicker in dark eyes
Sorrow, the restless wind
A wolf howl to the skies

© John Henson

****

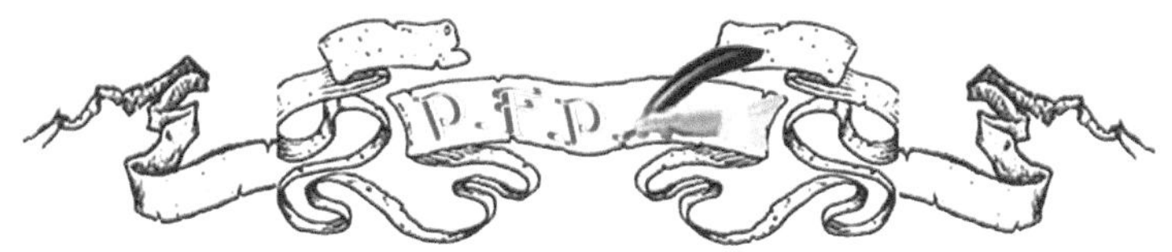

John W. Henson

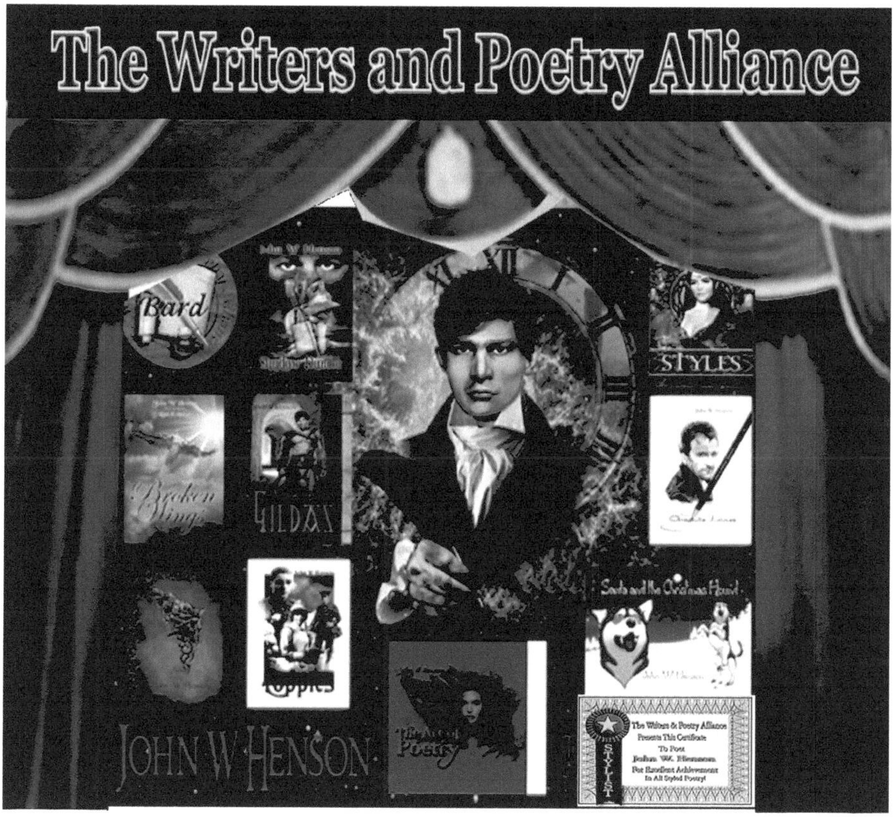

The Writers and Poetry Alliance

http://www.apfpublisher.com/others.html

****

I Remember

(Starter Poem 7)

I walk this forest in dreams meandering
In the clearing the ancient stones still stand
I feel the pull of my soul surrendering
To another time in this strange land

The night draws in on these silent witnesses
The shadows grow long as mists descend
Through vapourous shrouds my mind regresses
To a bygone age where the two worlds blend

I feel again the leathern hilt against my palm
I see the ancient futharks deep graven rune
Keeping me safe by the power of mystic charm
Carved in reverence to the lady of the moon

Silent movement parts the gossamer threads
A ghostly maiden stands there before my eyes
Her diaphanous gown blown in moonlit shreds
Reflecting the starlight of these ageless skies

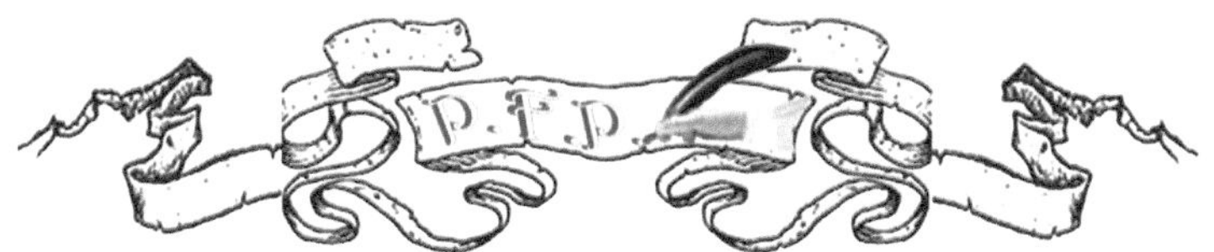

Words float upon the breeze, the air imbue
And my heart becomes a glowing ember
I hear in the ancient tongue ‘fien seac tu’
I hear the music of her voice and I remember

© John Henson

****

Forest Dreams

Forest

dreams of another time

Her gown reflects starlight

Ancient stones stand in reverence

To the silent lady of the night

© John Henson

****

Mystic Charm

In dreams I feel

The mystic charm

Of ancient bygone age

Meandering I feel ghostly

As I float like music

© Patricia Ann Farnsworth-Simpson

****

Forest Dreams

Forest dreams another time,
Mystic charm keeping safe,
Ageless skies ghostly maiden,
Remember music of her heart,
Upon a breeze

© Christina R Jussaume

****

Meandering Dreams

Meandering dreams reflecting
ghostly in the moon throughout
the ageless skies,
surrendering the mystic shadows
of a graven rune.

© Erich J. Goller

****

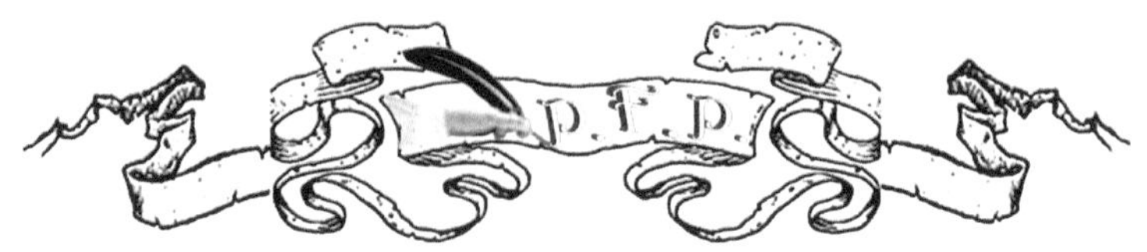

Mystical Reflections

Rune of mystic power
Reflecting starlight
On the gossamer threads
Of a ghostly maiden
In her diaphanous gown

© George L. Ellison

****

Ancient Threads

I hear
I feel
I see
I walk
I float
in shadows
my shrouds
in shreds
of ancient threads

© Dena M. Ferrari

****

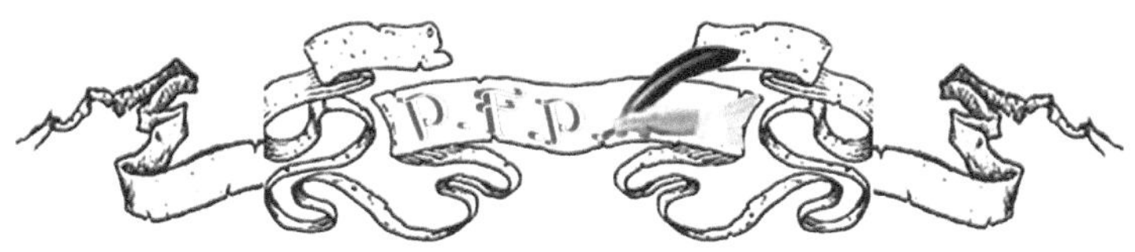

Rune Carved Worlds

I walk the night
The mists blend
In the moonlight
Silent reverence
of the dreams grow
By rune carved worlds

© Dena M. Ferrari

****

Ancient Power

Remember
meandering
as ghostly
night witnesses
reverence,
surrendering
to ancient mystic power.

© Janet L. Vick

****

Societies Child

(Starter Poem 8)

A ragged boy in ragged clothes
Bloodied knees and snotty nose
Looking for someone to care
A latchkey kid Mum's never there

On the streets all hours of the night
Strangers call he no longer takes flight
Every hooker on the street knows
The tough kid in the scruffy clothes

Then he meets a kindly man
Gives him food he eats all he can
So quick it was just a groan
A scared little boy died all alone

Mum is distraught is wasn't her fault
It was the drink you see she couldn't halt
His Father well! Not there you see
Because Mum didn't know who he could be

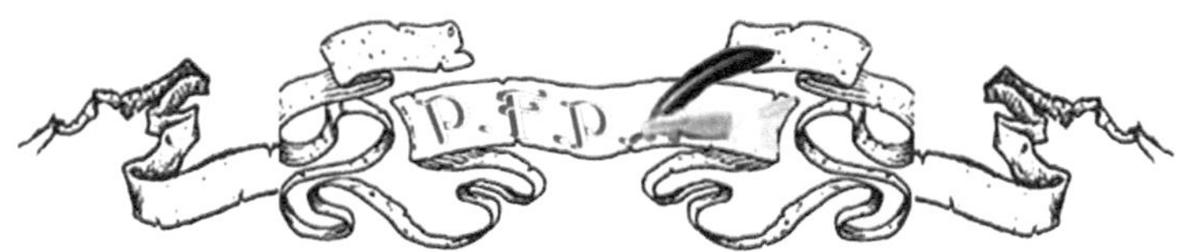

The kindly man enters his plea
He's not responsible, how could he be
It was just a street kid I mean to say
He's not to blame, he's just made that way

And every Sunday we kneel and pray
Then we do nothing to God's dismay
We're not responsible we're so meek and mild
He wasn't our's he was societies child

© John W. Henson

****

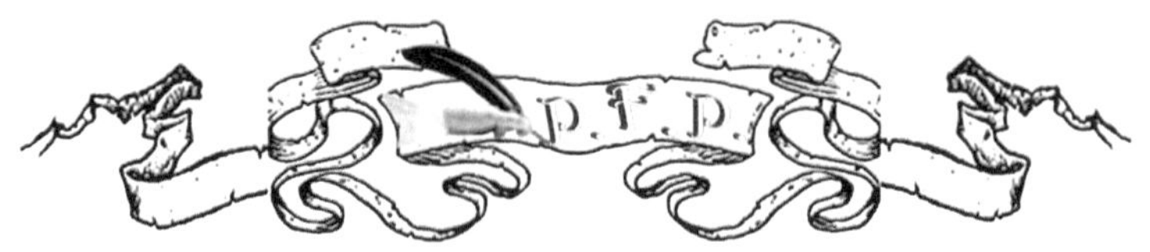

Someone to Drink

Strangers in the night
Looking to the streets in flight
The hooker, scared, alone
Died so quick, just a groan

© John W. Henson

****

All Alone

His Mum and Father
did not care,
Scared on the street
all alone in the night
the little boy died.

© Erich J. Goller

****

The Street Kid

Latchkey kid on night streets

Scared tough little kid

Distraught hooker Mum

We do nothing for

Society's child, not ours

© Christina R Jussaume

****

Societies Responsible

Father in drink

Mum distraught

Boy alone to groan

To kindly man

He gives plea

Societies responsible

You see

© Patricia Ann Farnsworth-Simpson

****

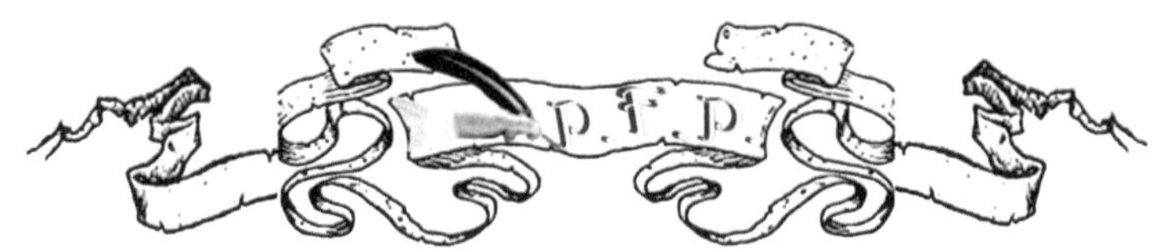

Street Kid

A street kid
Bloodied, scared
In scruffy clothes
Died alone
God and mum despair
For societies child
Who is responsible?

© George L. Ellison

****

Senryu

responsible blame
every ragged father
God's Sunday bloodied

societies scared
because we're snotty strangers
fault looking kindly

© Janet L. Vick

****

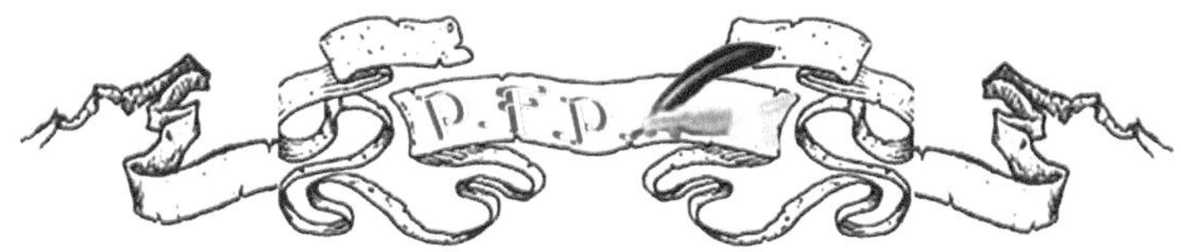

Janet L. Vick

http://apfpublisher.com/Janet.html

****

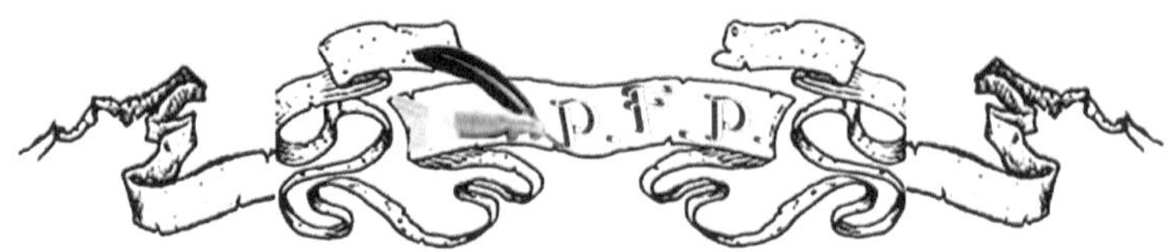

Celebration Dress-up

(Starter Poem 9)

I will be dressed as Goofie's twin
as the character seems to fit.
Never could walk in these high heels,
I stagger like someone who's lit.

Dress was a pink prom fantasy
since that's what it was way back when.
But though they prayed while cleaning it,
fantasy's changed into pumpkin.

I worry 'bout the eye make-up
'cause it sort of comes out in clots.
So just pretend they're fake lashes
and artfully tied into knots.

With hair bleached by sun, wind and dirt,
of style...it just hangs in a tail...
Tried fixing with teases and curls,
then mirror flashed sign out 'for sale'.

Yes, I'm coming, I will be there,
the staggering orange twin Goofie.
I talk with a drawl, Southernese
So party, get ready for me!

© Janet Vick

****

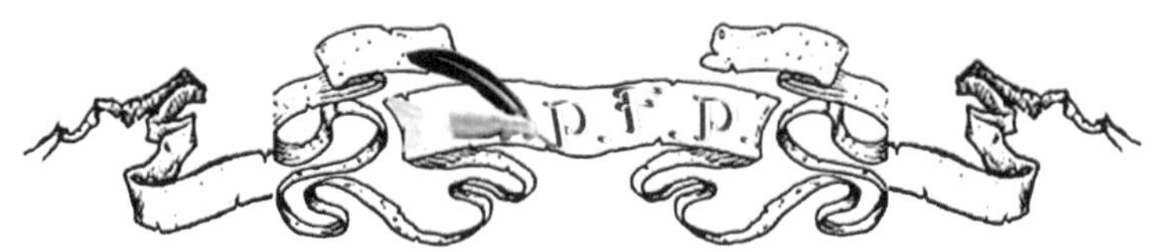

The Twin

It seems
twin never changed style...
High,
staggering into the party,
fake drawl,
dressed in fantasy.

© Janet Vick

****

I Could

I could pretend to
stagger like Goofie
and talk with a drawl
Dressed in a style like a
fantasy character

© Dena M. Ferrari

****

I Pretend

To party staggering in style

Hair bleached fake lashes high heels

I pretend Southernese drawl

No pumpkin will I be

© Patricia Ann Farnsworth-Simpson

****

Goofy

Artfully bleached hair character

with a goofie staggering

high heels walk and

ready dressed for a fantasy's

prom party.

© Erich J. Goller

****

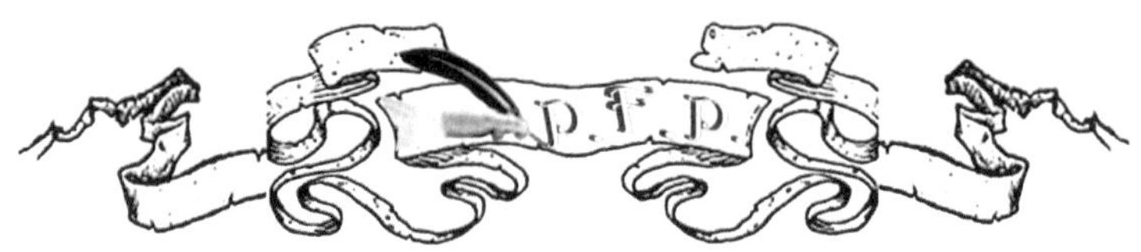

Out of Character

She dressed
with fantasy
in artful pink with heels.
The prom hung in fake teasing knots…
just dirt.

© Karen O'Leary

****

Fantasy Dressed

In fantasy dressed
In party pink dress
Staggering high heels
And sun bleached hair
All tied in knots

© Peter Duggan

****

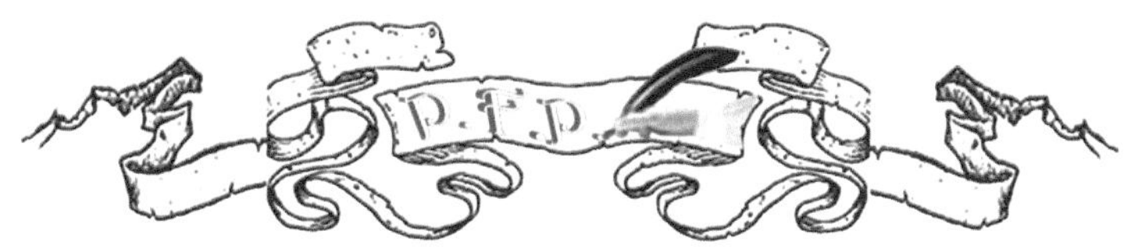

Get Ready to Party

Character was fit in
pink prom dress and heels
make-up, pretend false lashes
and bleached hair - the mirror tried…

© Rhoda Galgiani

****

It Comes Through

A fantasy character
lit from the mirror
With a walk and talk
It comes through
to pretend
it was me

© Dena M. Ferrari

****

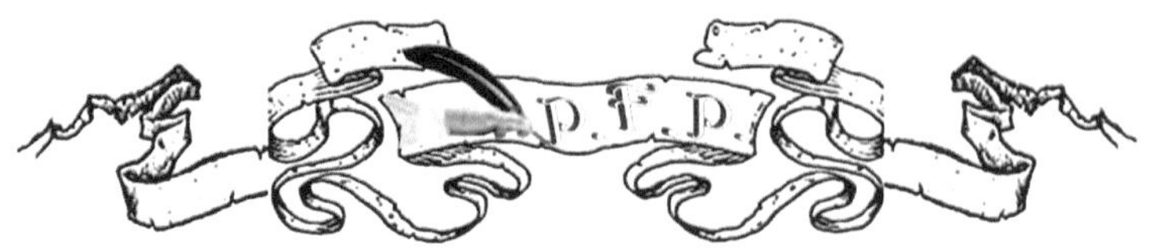

Prom Fantasy

Dressed in high heels I stagger
Pumpkin dress with bleached hair
Goofie's twin tried artfully
Ready party, yes I'm coming

© Christina R Jussaume

****

Join Me

Bleached hair,
Lashes fake,
Pink dress.
Heels so high
I stagger when I walk.
I'm ready,
Party with me.

© Sue White

****

Sue White

The Writers and Poetry Alliance
Sue
White
The Writers And Poetry Alliance
Scribe

****

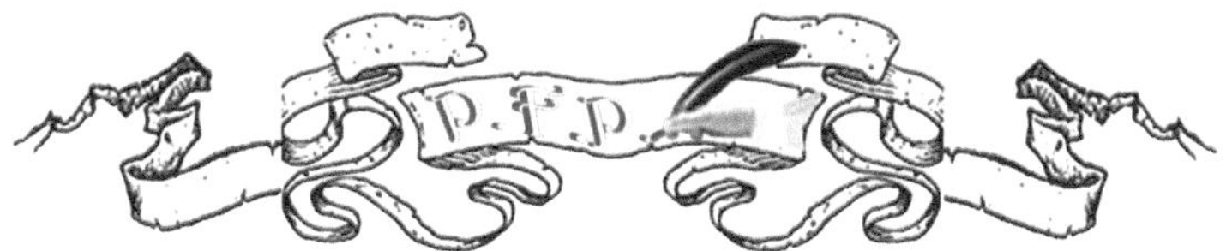

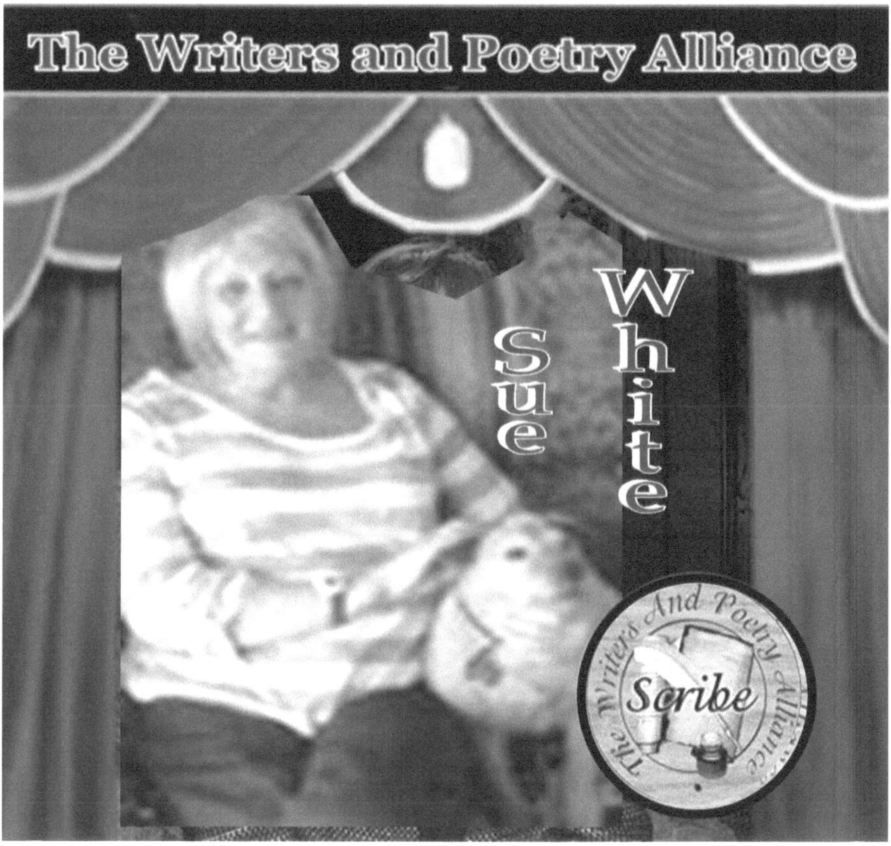

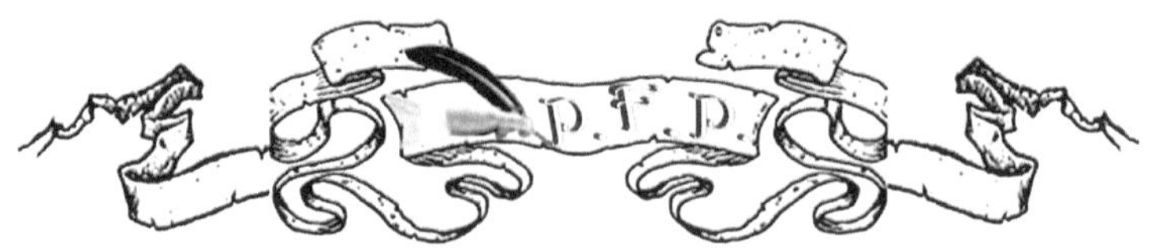

Within These Walls

(Starter Poem 10)

I gaze around in awe
This house now mine I close the door
A wreak of a house left years ago
Still feeling the love it embraces me so.

It beckoned me come near, come near
It beckoned me to come, come live here
I shall keep you safe within my walls
As I have done before, it calls.

I walked around the empty rooms
Across old worn boards on the second floor
Now I ascend the creaking stairs to the attic door
Slowly easing open the gloom cut by a shaft of light
My eye's accustoming to the sight.

In the corner hidden in a shadow an old chest left behind
Abandoned, forgotten or left for someone to find.

Carefully unwrapping as I unpack
Yesterdays scent comes wafting back.

A fragile beautiful piece of lace

Once hiding happiness, love, hope on someone's face.

A gilded frame the photo now a bluer.

A heart shaped locket with a strand of hair.

Stirring of emotion rediscovering lost secret’s of this place.

I now understand why this house beckoned me to embrace

It wanted me to feel its love of the past.

I have found my peace here to put down roots and stay at last.

© Sue White

****

Yesterday

Her scent on fragile lace

Strands of grey hair upon her face

Secret's, emotion embrace

Yesterday's love in this place.

© Sue White

****

Yesterdays Sight

Behind the attic door

around a hidden corner

a forgotten photo of yesterday

unwrapping yesterdays sight

for happiness and love.

© Erich J. Goller

****

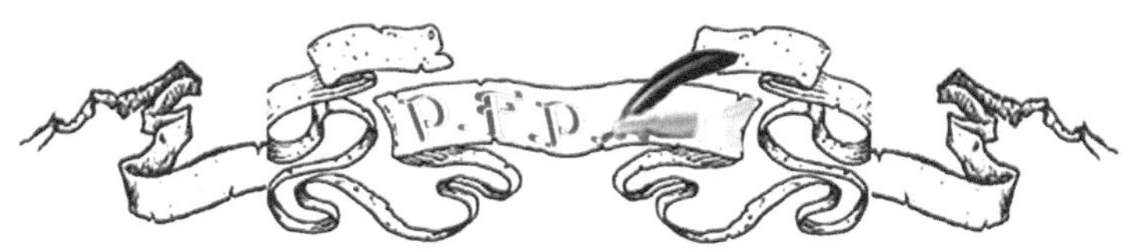

Beckoned Come

As emotion embraces
the forgotten yesterdays,
love calls... Come.

Fragile, hope hiding,
open carefully.
Peace beckoned... Come.

© Janet L. Vick

****

Come Live With Me

Safe I shall keep you
This house it's mine
Come live with me
Peace here to find

© Peter Duggan

****

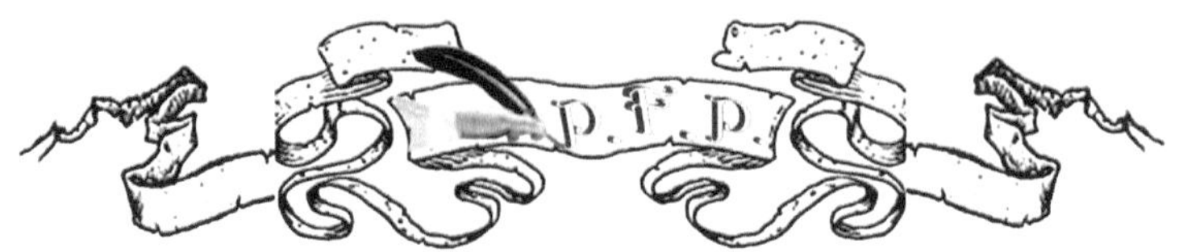

The Locket

A scent of fragile emotions
Carefully hiding
left by someone's face
Within my hands a
heart shaped locket
I embrace

© George L. Ellison

****

Yesterdays Happiness

House I love embraces me
beckoned calls, live here
yesterdays embrace me
feel the love of the past -
my roots

© Rhoda Galgiani

****

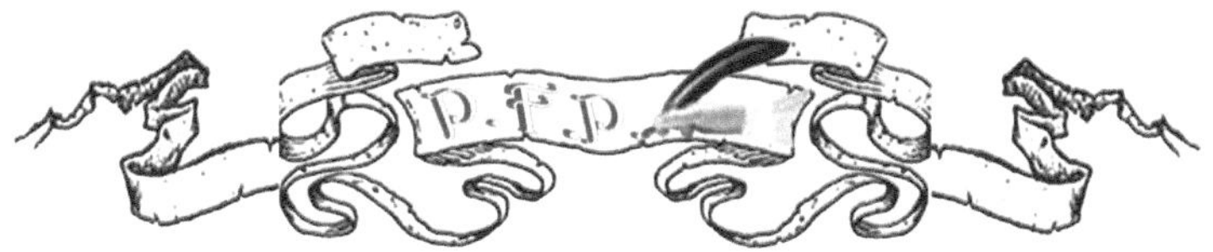

Rhoda Galgiani

http://www.apfpublisher.com/chesakat.html

****

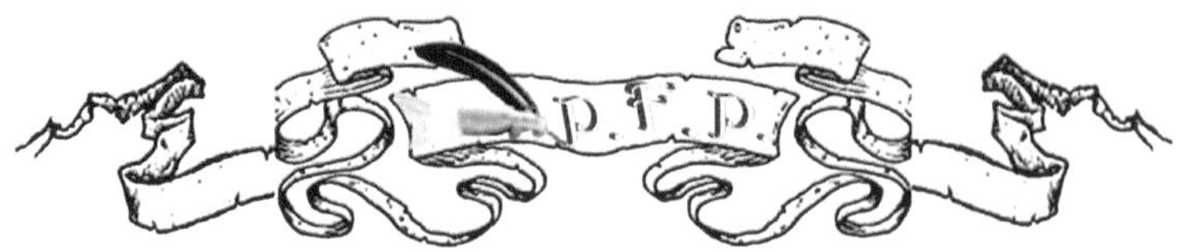

Turning the Page

(Starter Poem 11)

There comes a time in ones life
when turning the page is needed to be
As imagination gathers upon ones soul
of thoughts as what should have been

All is well deep within, but the emptiness
that lingers takes its toll and sadness cries
Weary of the darkened cloud above the brow
one struggles to clear the heart and mind

Time is a healer as one comes to grips
with the woes buried in ones lining
Quiet simple thoughts console the spirit
comforting the grief carried in a sad heart

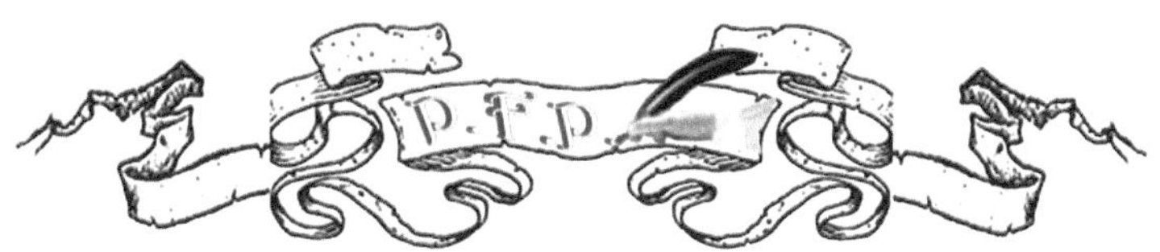

Change to the minds thought of solitude
is rendered as a gift from worlds beyond
The gift will bring well being a gift that
will heal the disarray of ones soul when
Sad moments choose to come into view

****

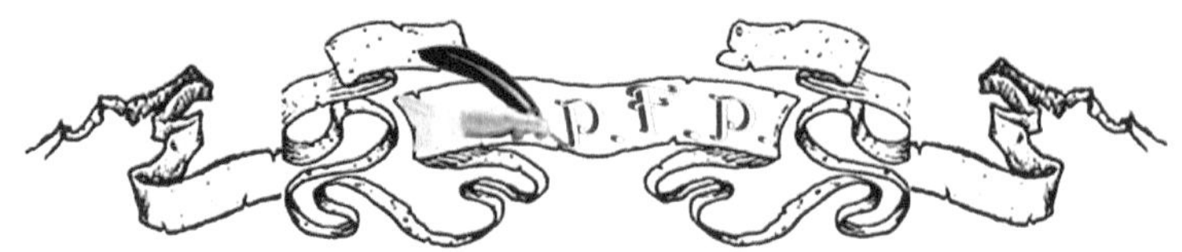

Ones Heart and Mind

Time - the healer

Quiet - consoles the spirit

Change - buried the woes

Life - a healer, a gift

Deep - from worlds beyond

© Rhoda Galgiani

****

Comforting Thoughts

A world emptiness

with sadness beyond

a darkened cloud

struggles to bring

clear comforting thoughts

to the heart and soul.

© Erich J. Goller

****

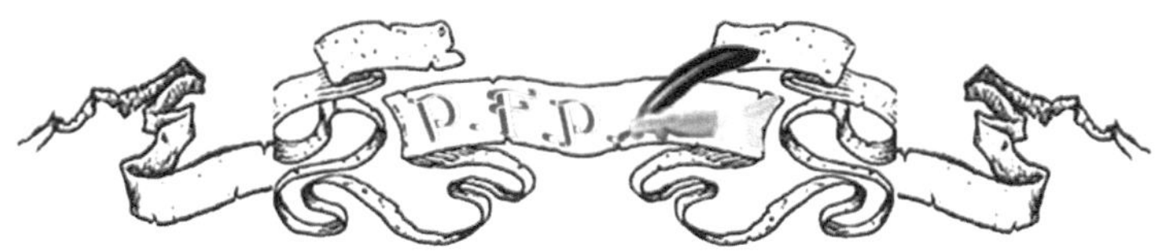

Life Is A Gift

Life is a gift
The soul within gathers
a deep and comforting heart
from beyond worlds

© Dena M. Ferrari

****

The Gift

time
turns…
pages
of sadness
change to solitude
as the Healer consoles the heart

© Karen O'Leary

****

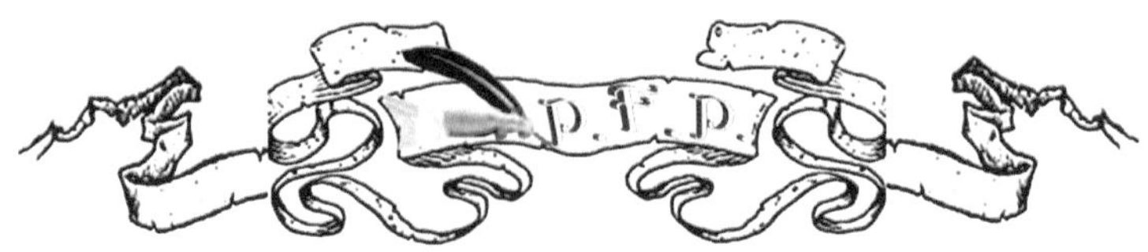

As Thoughts Come

As thoughts come
comforting grief,
heart struggles,
cries emptiness
and lingers.
Spirit buried,
weary within sadness toll.

© Janet L. Vick

****

Solitude Gathers

Deep within emptiness
Comes to grips with the grief
As solitude gathers in sadness
The weary heart takes its toll

© Patricia Ann Farnsworth-Simpson

****

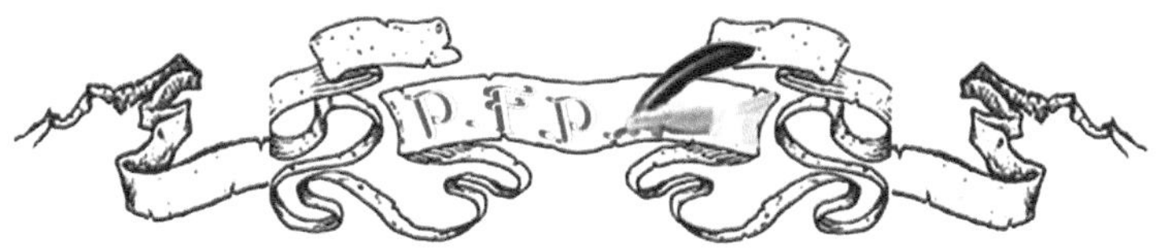

A Healer Comes

Emptiness lingers
from a soul in the well
A healer comes from beyond the cloud
deep within the needed imagination

****

Struggles

A healer and a page
buried a Spirit of Time

One soul in a well
struggles with the grief

****

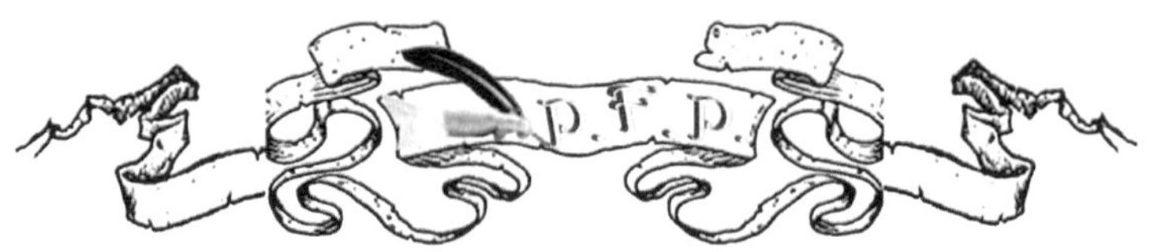

Clear The Mind

In solitude
Choose the cloud
Moments of imagination,
Change the mind,
Different view
Heart clear
Gift carried by the soul.

© Sue White

****

Emptiness

Deep within is emptiness
And sadness of the mind
Imagination gift of thoughts
Takes its toll

© Peter Duggan

****

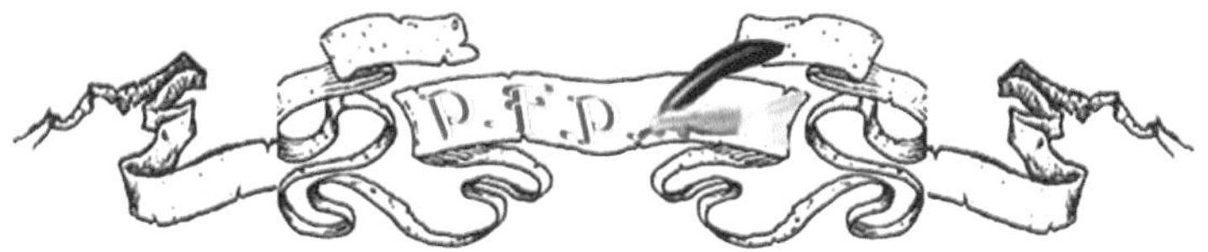

Peter Duggan

http://apfpublisher.com/pedro.html

****

Turn On Your Light

(Starter Poem 12)

Turn on your light
Light the velvet softness of your night
You might have felt that breath of sweetest power
In that silver moon
That paints the twilight hours
Have you ever felt that mystic pull
That takes you from the smallest flower
To melt into the all.

I sometimes stand there staring at the sea
As each wave reaches out to destiny
To fade and then to come back
So another wave might form
To be destroyed
Then to be reborn….

Turn on your light
Pass no judgment, who’s to say what’s right?
No need for this when light is shining bright

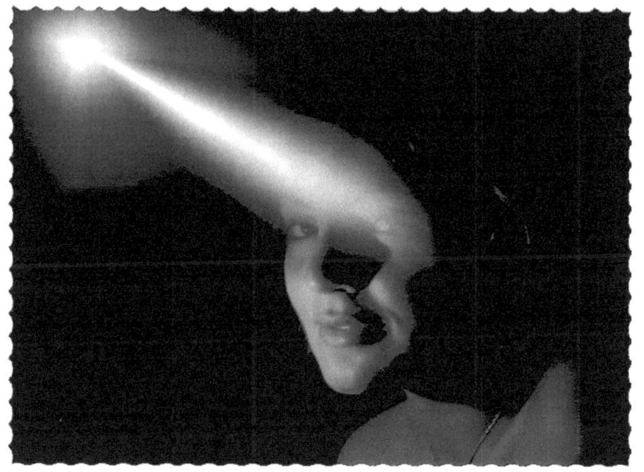

Have you felt such magic
Have you felt that pull
It's something that must happen to each fool
He must learn how to melt into
The silence of the all.

The secrets they be wrote within your soul
Seek them out and let them make you whole
Each flower it must bloom then die
So know your precious I
Must be destroyed
To be reborn…

****

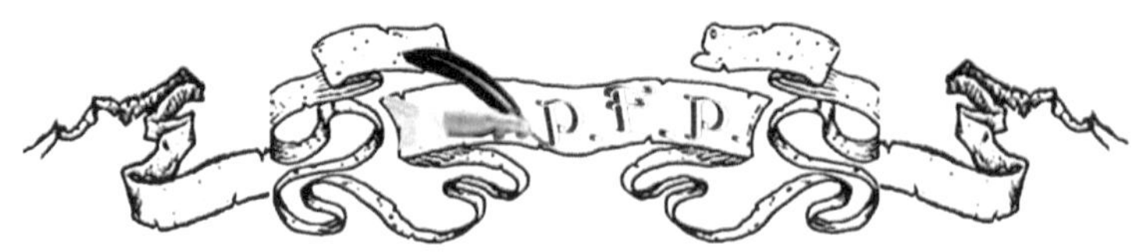

That Precious Light

The softness of the light
Is shining bright
In the sweetness of the night
That precious light

© Peter Duggan

****

Silver Moon Night

The sweetest softness within
the flower soul shining bright
in the magic of the silent silver
moon night hours.

© Erich J. Goller

****

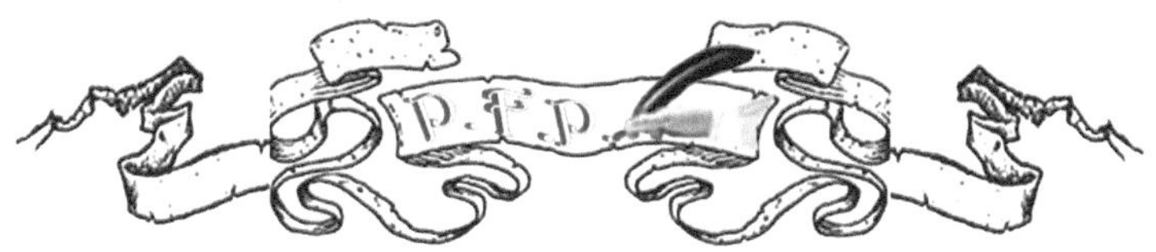

Like a Flower

Like a flower
The velvet softness of your soul
Reaches out for the light
To bloom and make you whole

© Patricia Ann Farnsworth-Simpson

****

Precious

The sweetest night with you
Takes power from judgment
I felt your mystic light
I learn your soul is precious

© Dena M. Ferrari

****

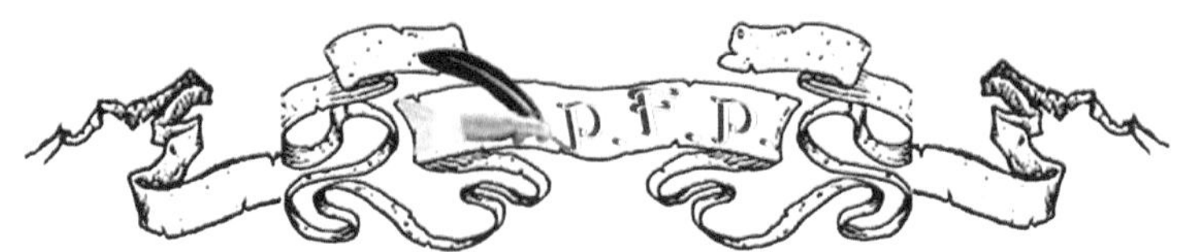

Twilight

(Whitney)

Night power...
Mystic twilight
reaches soul,
sweetest silence.
Secrets melt,
reborn in light
that destiny paints as whole.

© Janet L. Vick

****

Light of the Night

Silver moon turn on your light
velvet power in twilight hours
mystic pull reaches flower -
must die to be reborn

© Rhoda Galgiani

****

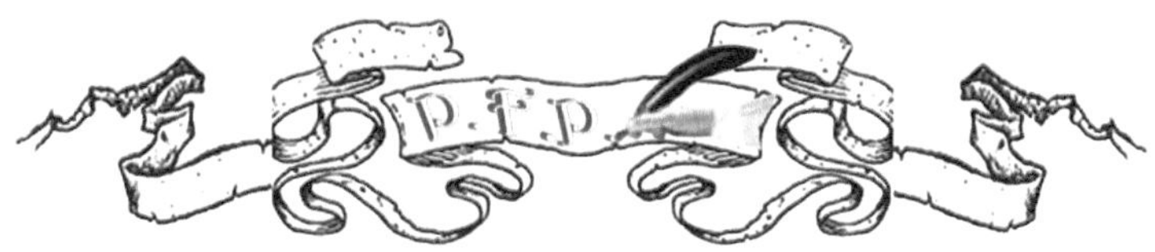

Precious Soul

Melt into silence,

Precious soul reborn

Magic pull of your light

No judgment pass,

Form destiny, as wave reaches out

© Christina R Jussaume

****

The Storm

Moon a silver light

Waves pounding

Breath held tight

No soul saved in the violence

Now just silence.

© Suc White

****

Walking the Wetlands

(Starter Poem 13)

The sky be filled with laughter
That echo's through the morn
I walk along this tree lined trail
Some hours after dawn
Loud Kookaburra, in tree top
Seems to know what life's about
He knows that it's all just a dance
Of this he has no doubt.

The sky so blue above my head
Seems to look at me and smile
As feather feet go trekking on
To cover bliss filled miles
As coloured parrots in a tree
Do screech in bold delight
The sun shines down on twisted trees
As the morning shines so bright.

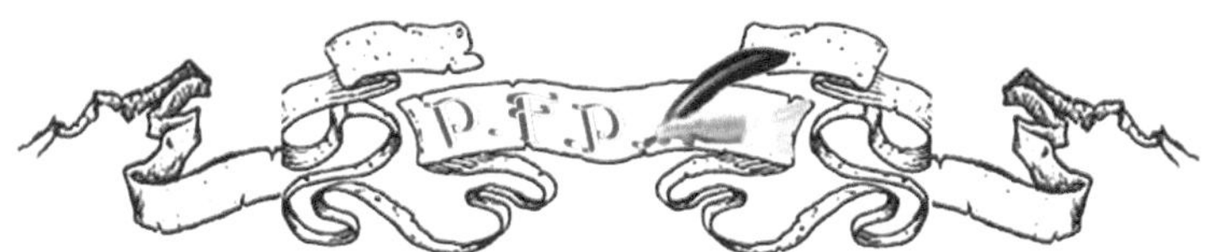

As lake reflecting golden sun
Shines back a million gems
Two Kangaroos, do cross my path
And I just look at them
And wonder at their magic forms
All muscular and grand
As I marvel at the beauty of
This lovely city's wetlands

© Peter Duggan

****

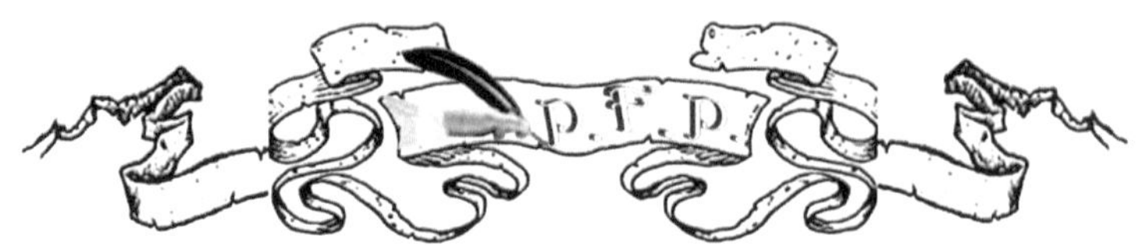

Dawns Delight

That coloured parrot in a tree

I look at it's wonder

As sun shines bright

The dawn, is a delight

© Peter Duggan

****

Golden Colored

The golden colored beauty of

the wetlands parrots trees

marvel in the morning bright

sunshine, that forms a magic path.

© Erich J. Goller

****

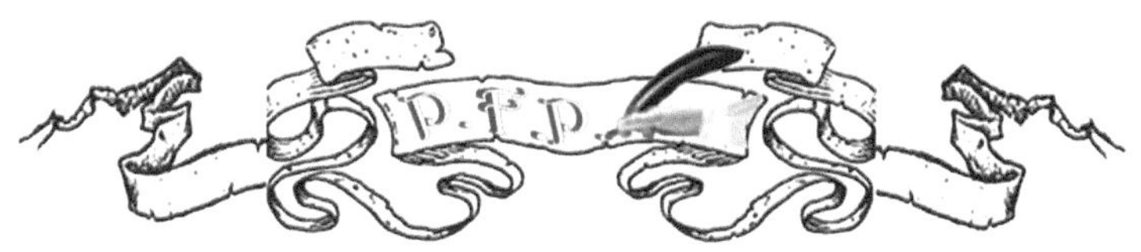

Magic Feather

The sky filled with a million parrots
A bright coloured feather
in my path
seems to be magic

© Dena M. Ferrari

****

Double Senyru

delight trekking morn
laughter shines, echoes life's dance
reflecting magic

feather beauty
dawn colored morning
wonder filled bliss

© Janet L. Vick

****

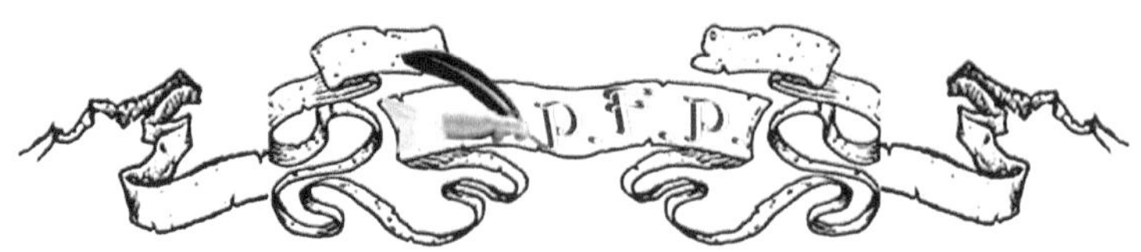

Dawn Awakes

Through dawn
Laughter echo's
A Kookaburra.

Sky reflecting
On the lake.
Magic,
Bliss.
Life's a dance.

© Sue White

****

I Dance

The loud screech above my head
echo's back
After miles I walk the path
through a magic trail
as I dance

© Dena M. Ferrari

****

The City's Wetlands

The sky echo's to me
beauty and delight as
twisted tree top reflecting
golden sun on the
city's wetlands - dance

© Rhoda Galgiani

****

Two Kangaroos

I look at two kangaroos
and marvel in delight
Their muscular beauty seems to shine
In the morning sun bright

© Patricia Ann Farnsworth-Simpson

****

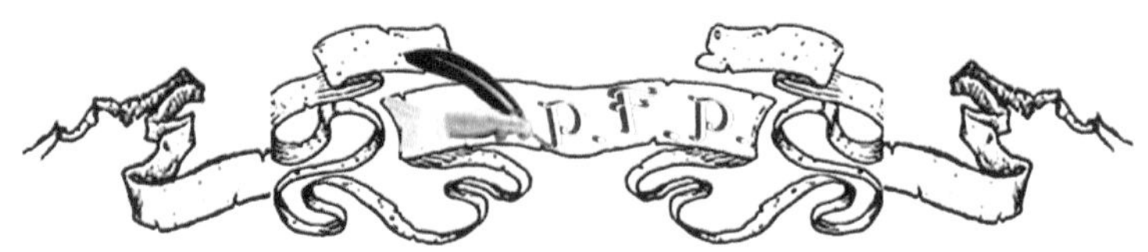

Morning of Delight

The trees dance about
Life's trail has a path
to a magic morning of delight
I walk with a smile

© Dena M. Ferrari

****

Trekking the Wetlands

miles
of bliss--
the sun shines
through grand twisted
trees

© Karen O'Leary

****

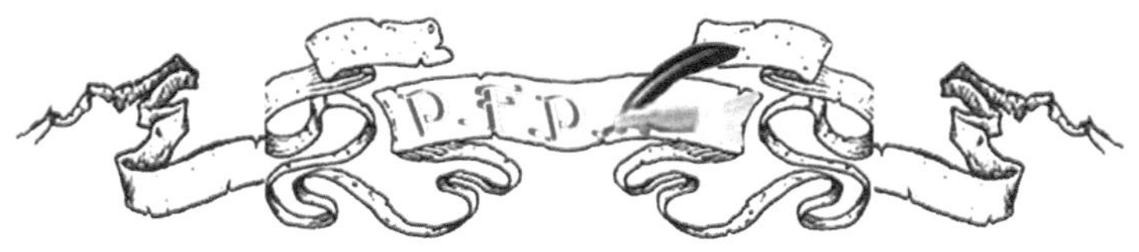

Karen O'Leary

http://www.apfpublisher.com/Karen.html

****

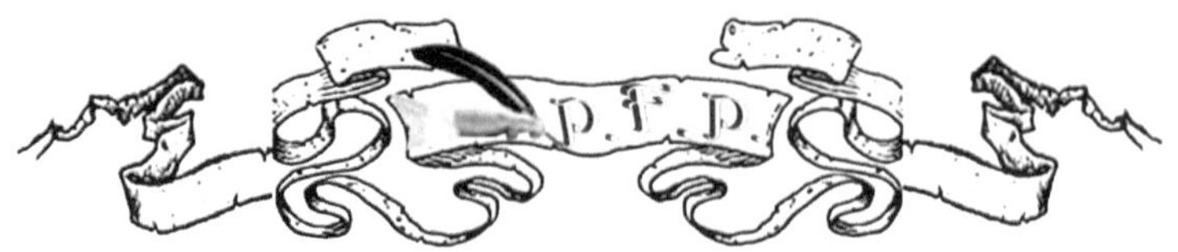

Liberation

(Starter Poem 14)

Open fields, unfettered
by walls and concrete
speak to my soul,
freeing my spirit to soar.

Green fields, uncluttered
by sandwiched buildings
touch my heart,
helping me to hope.

Natural fields, untainted
by industries' greed
clear my mind,
daring me to dream.

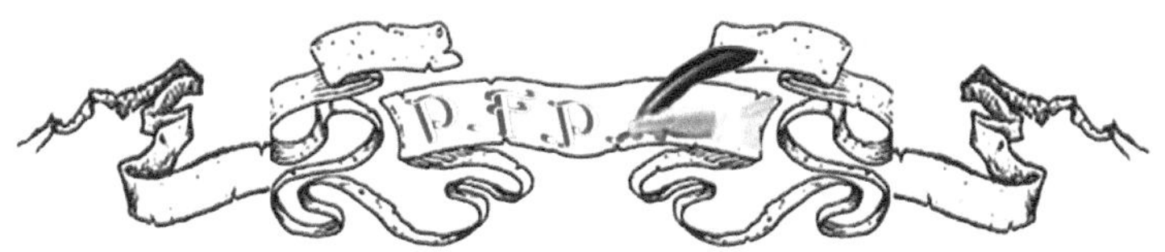

Flower-sprinkled fields, unsoiled

by strewn litter

enchant my eyes

giving me a glimpse of God.

© Karen O'Leary

****

God Speaks…

clearing
the concrete walls…
my soul, liberated
by God, soars untainted to hope
and dream

© Karen O'Leary

****

Daring Dream

Open natural flower fields,
a clear sprinkled uncluttered soul
soars to freeing a daring dream
of hope to touch God.

© Erich J. Goller

****

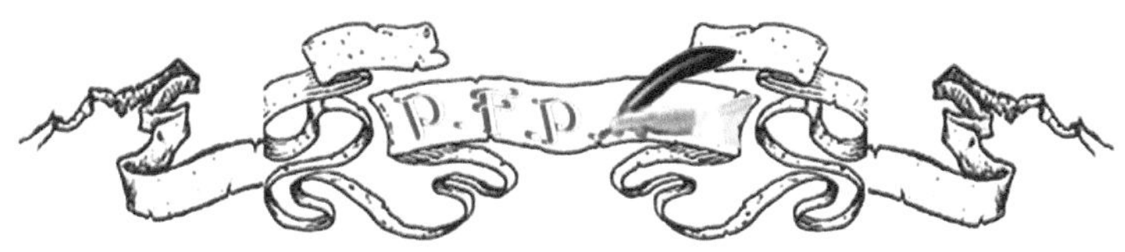

My Untainted Soul

My untainted soul
My unsoiled mind
My unfettered spirit
My uncluttered heart
My dream of hope
Enchant me

© Dena M. Ferrari

****

Giving Me Hope

Unfettered my soul and eyes dream
Glimpses of God to enchant me
Helping to clear my mind
Giving me hope!

© Patricia Ann Farnsworth-Simpson

****

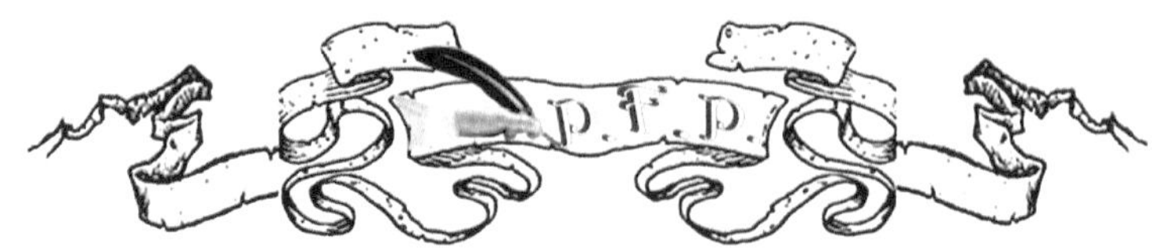

Open Heart

Unfettered hope,

opened heart,

uncluttered mind.

Giving soul

to God.

© Janet L. Vick

****

Urban Greed

Buildings.
Walls.
Concrete.
Greed.
Litter.
A glimpse of fields green,
My dream.
Give my spirit hope God.

© Sue White

****

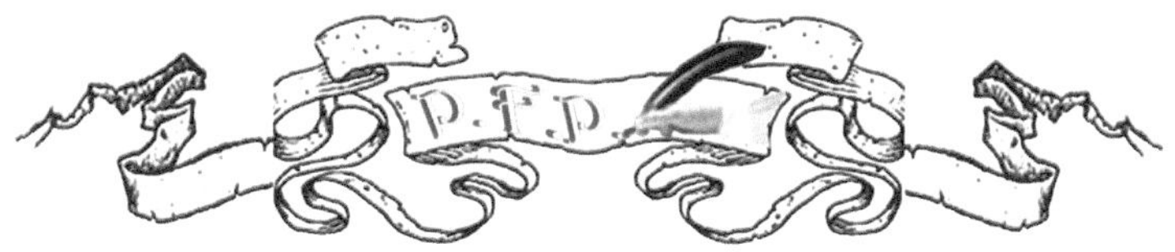

Kevin Bates

The Writers & Poetry Alliance

Blacpanther

Laureate

Kevin Bates

http://www.apfpublisher.com/Kevin.html

****

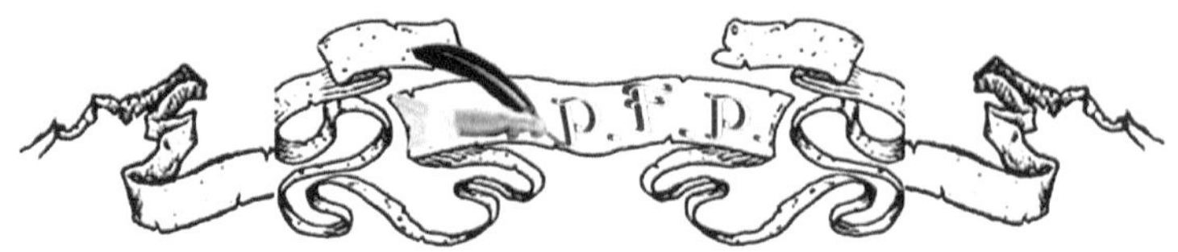

Tip Toe

(Starter Poem 15)

It's now the big party night
what everyone been waiting for.
You and I have made eye contact
circle the room to find each other.

Stand there with drinks in hand;
talking about happens in our life.
Many would call it small talk
yet it is humongous for you & I.

Party is now coming to a close
a few has had too much to drink.
My knees wobble I take a stumble
I'm sure it's not the wine it's you.

Put others up in the bedrooms;
lay me down gently on the couch.
Time pass I'm sure everyone is sleep;
I then tip toe down the hallway.

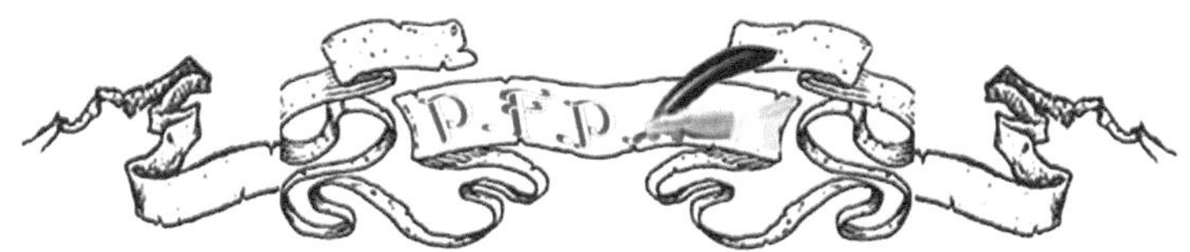

So careful as not to disturb nobody,
my business with you is our concern.
Knock so gently on your bedroom door
Greeted with an alluring smile and kiss.

****

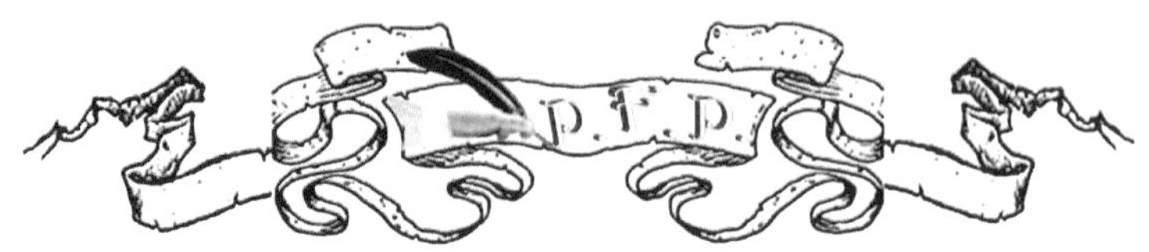

A Kiss Happens

Greeted with your
alluring hand.
I then wobble;
time pass with
you and I.
Then a kiss happens

© Kevin Bates

****

Alluring Kiss

I have had to many drinks,
tip toe I wobble in the hallway
to your bedroom for
your alluring kiss.

Erich J. Goller

****

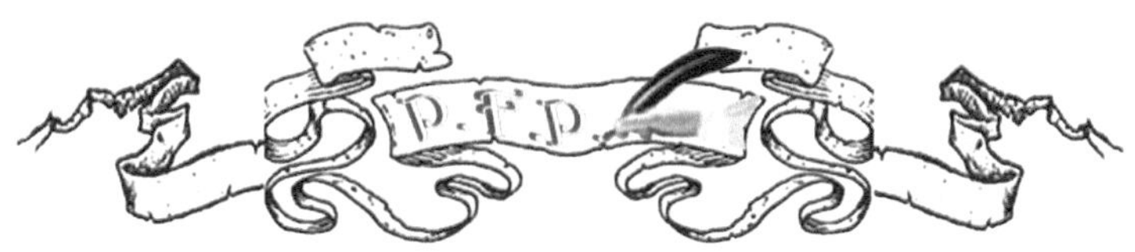

Party Circle

A party circle...
Talking,
drinks wobble,
stumble happens...
Nobody down
Yet.
Drink close....

© Janet Vick

****

You and I

Gently

You and I kiss

Others stand in circle

I take your hand

With a smile

© Dena M. Ferrari

****

Careful

Careful,
disturb not…
alluring kiss
put everyone to sleep.

Concern for nobody
as gentle life
lay down with drink.

© Janet L.Vick

****

Lust at First Sight

We circle the room
Eye contact is made
An alluring smile
Small talk, a drink
Your bedroom, a kiss

© George L. Ellison

****

George L. Ellison

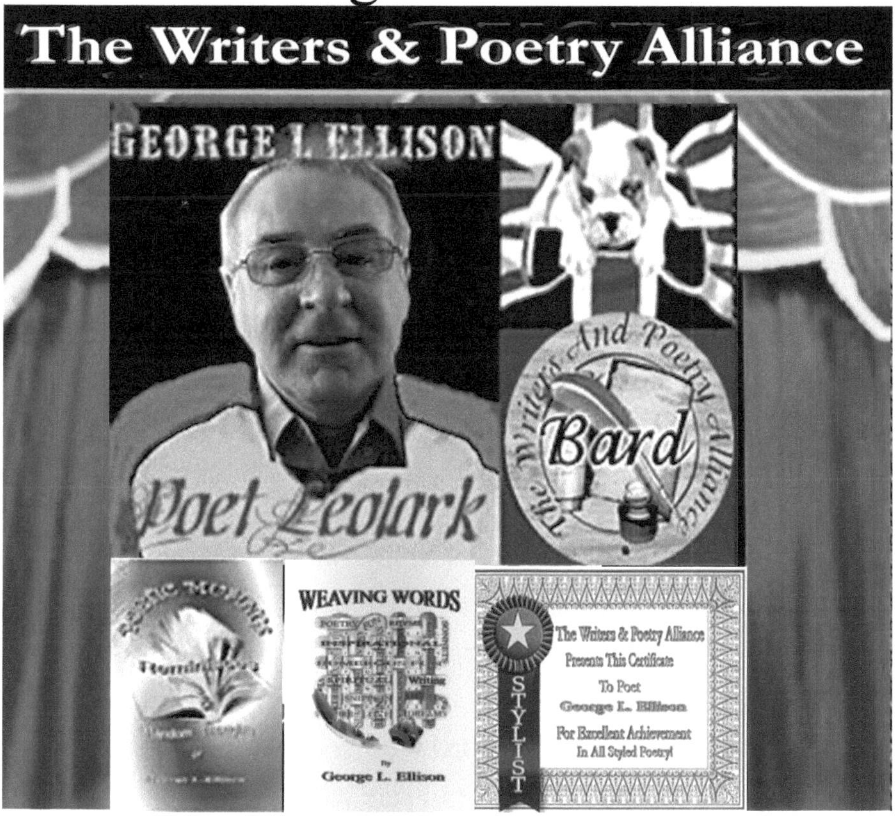

The Writers & Poetry Alliance

AKA

Poet Leolark

http://apfpublisher.com/leolark.html

****

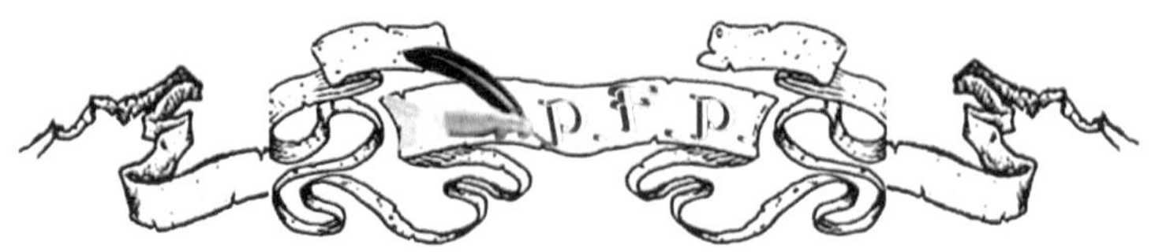

Reminiscence

(Starter Poem 16)

The Pace of life can be so fast
Tight schedules can make one gasp
So given the chance I let the pores exude
The feeling of utter solitude
To take time out, let my thoughts just fly
Allow the day to pass me by
To go at my pace just for once
Ease my soul and let my thoughts bounce

Around my head they bob and weave
As all around me I perceive
The rustling leaves the trickling stream
The scented air and the sunlit scene
To look around the woodland glade
As the trials of life are allowed to fade
To think of nought but what I see
A falling leaf, a quivering tree

Many years ago it was all like this
We had the time we were at peace
But all that changed with this new age
Time sped up with each turning page

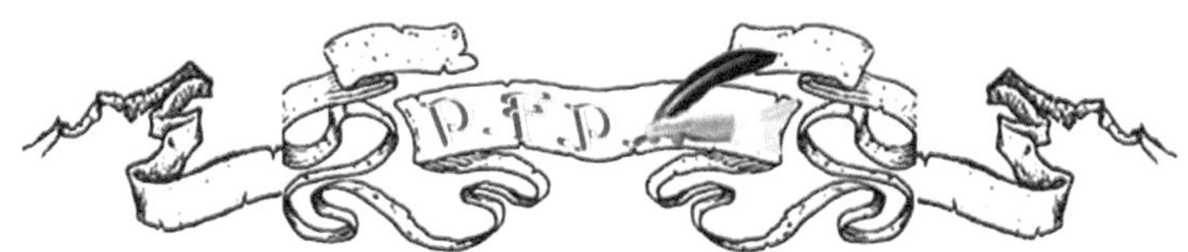

I yearn to be in yesterday
It now seems oh so far away
When we all had time for everyone
And looked forward to the rising sun

To set a pace we'd all enjoy
Each man and woman, girl and boy
To love thy neighbour as thyself
To lend a hand not keep to oneself
But the wheel of life rolls on and on
As we all head for the setting sun
So I take my chances so I don't miss
My times of solitude and bliss

© G. L. Ellison

****

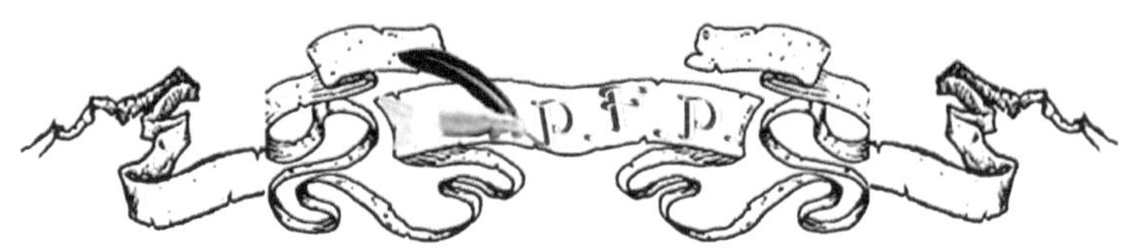

Solitude and Bliss

I sit
I perceive
Solitude

I enjoy
Feeling
Bliss

As my thoughts
Bob and weave

My soul is
At peace

© George L. Ellison

****

Life Trials

Time turning the page forward
as life trails quivering and rolls
to pass all the thoughts
with the setting sun.

© Erich J. Goller

****

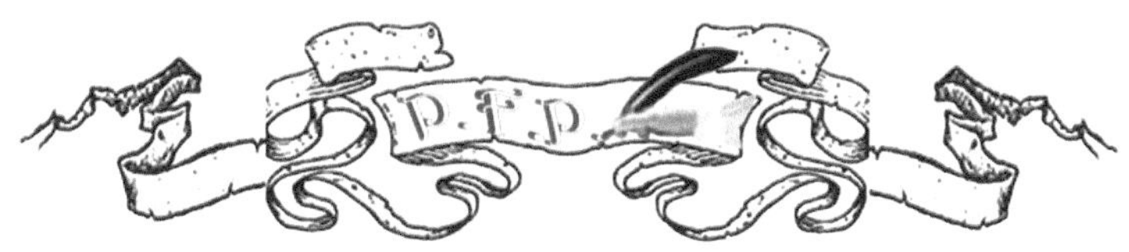

I Gasp for Air

Yesterday was the time

I see life fade

I gasp for air

Feeling the tight hand

Around my soul

© Dena M. Ferrari

****

A Katuata

time stream, wheel of chance

as pace rolls fast trickling life

thoughts weave peace with solitude

© Janet L. Vick

****

Bliss

Sun rising,
Solitude,
Peace.
Sunlit woodland.
Stream trickling on
Sped up the pace
To weave and bob around the glade.
Bliss.

© Sue White

****

The Wheel of Life

Trickling stream
and scented air
so many years ago
take time out
toward the new age -
thoughts for my peace

© Rhoda Galgiani

****

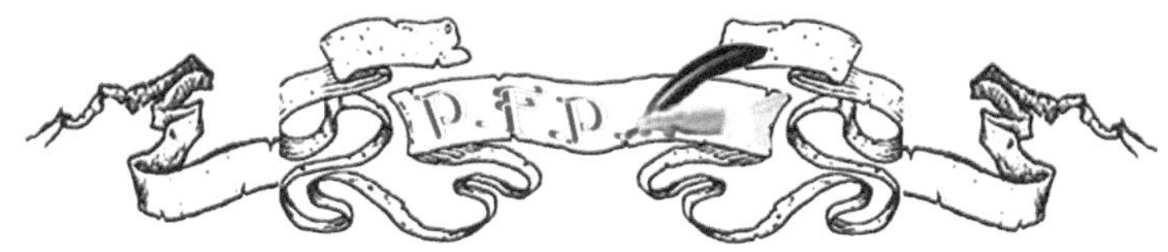

This I miss

Peace and solitude

And bliss

My soul to ease

This I miss

© Peter Duggan

****

Ease My Life

The rising sun
The trickling stream
The rustling leaves
The woodland glade
A quivering tree
Can ease my life

© Dena M. Ferrari

****

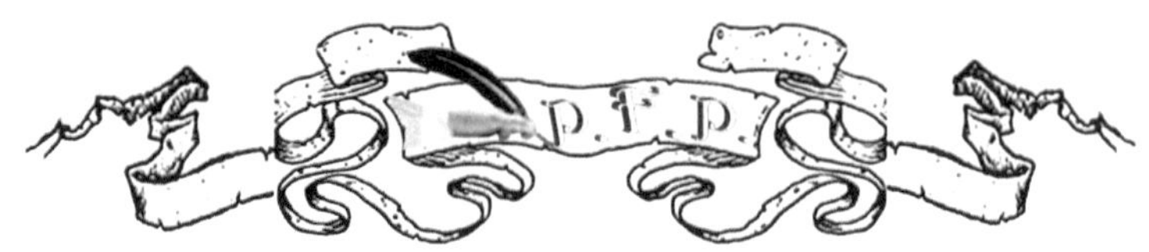

A Page Turning

peace

trickling

like a stream…

time of rising

sun

© Karen O'Leary

****

Falling

Falling…
Out of bliss

Quivering…
In solitude.

Yearn…
For the woman
I love.

© Kevin Bates

****

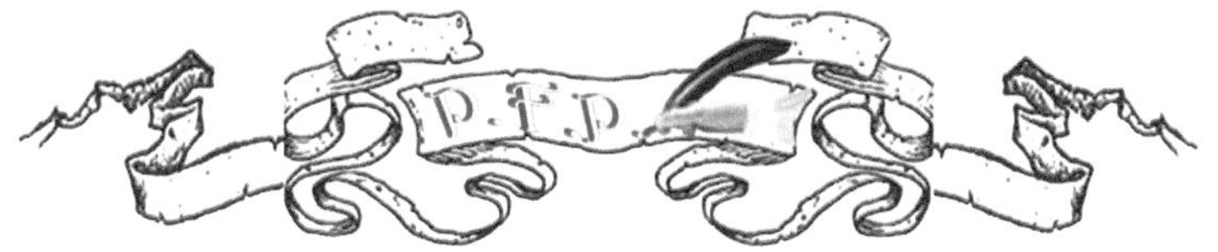

Sheri Stanley

The Writers & Poetry Alliance

Sheri Stanley

Poet Shesta

THE MORNING DREAM

Self-Portrait In Pastels

The Writers And Poetry Alliance

Wordsmith

****

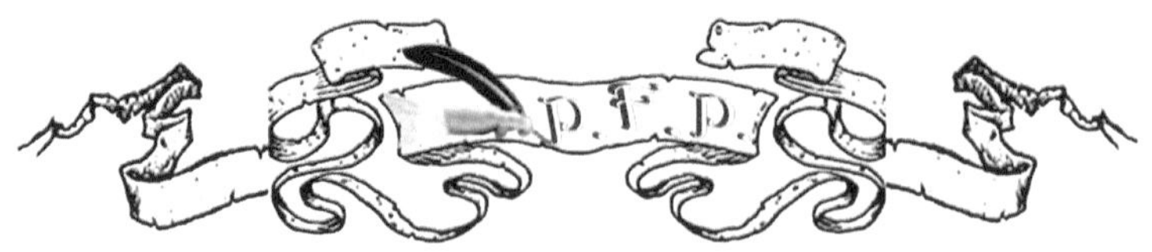

In Giving Thanks

(Starter Poem 17)

Sometimes there are days which seem empty

At times there are days oh, so full!

Yet, when days are so empty, a rainbow appears

Or a Hummingbird flies by and my heart cheers!

Some nights seem so terribly lonely

But, just for a moment or two,

Because I think of dear Jesus, who died on the cross,

And suffered for me and for you!

Do remember to count all your blessings!

These words can't be counted as trite

Your family, your friends and the love that it sends,

Make all sorrows seem small; life is bright!

Don't allow small things to be big ones!

Don't fall in that miserable trap

He died on the cross to pay for our sins

To live otherwise gives Him a slap!

Glory to God in His mercy and goodness!

Say thanks for another day!

Give praise to the One who adores you,

In love and in grace; it shows on your face!

****

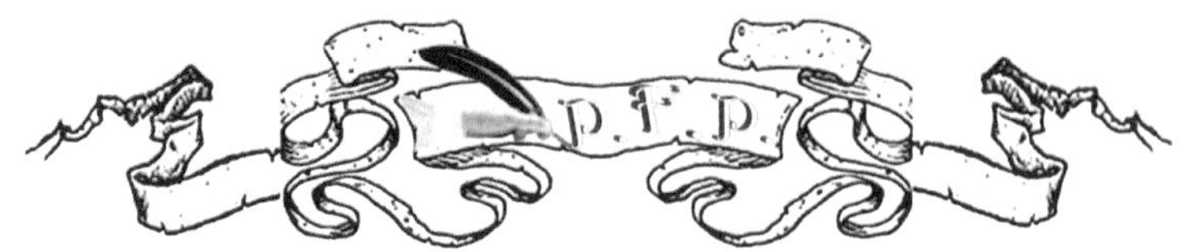

In The Rainbow

When a rainbow appears
I think of Jesus

Sorrows seem small
Words are trite; life is bright!

© Sheri Stanley

****

Rainbows Heart

Remember the lonely, empty
days and nights,
and the love I send for you,
a rainbows heart.

© Erich J. Goller

****

Rainbow Days

Rainbow days

A Hummingbird.

No sorrows

Heart full of love.

Bright is life.

Cheers to my family and friends.

© Sue White

****

Rainbow Days

Bright

in grace…

God's mercy

and love for me.

His blessings and grace live in my full heart.

© Karen O'Leary

****

Give Thanks

Give thanks

to Jesus.

Live love,

His grace shows.

© Janet L. Vick

****

Love is a Blessing

Give your heart full of love

To the one who adores you

Life gives rainbow moments

Love is a blessing

© Dena M. Ferrari

****

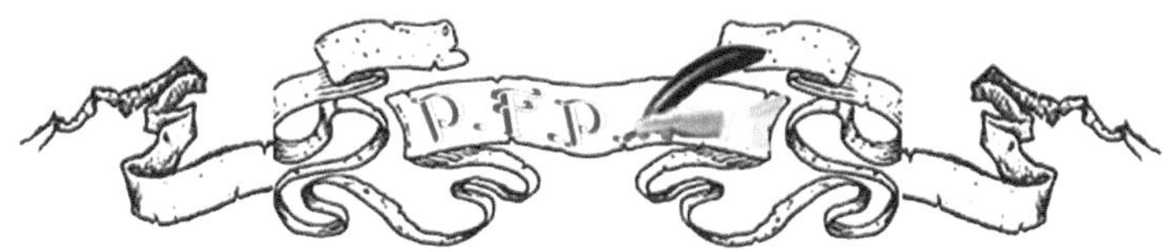

Sometimes

Sometimes life seems lonely
And days so empty
But God adores you
Praise be to him
For another day

© Peter Duggan

****

Remember

Don't allow
Don't fall
Do remember
Times so small
In just a moment
You are
in love

© Dena M. Ferrari

****

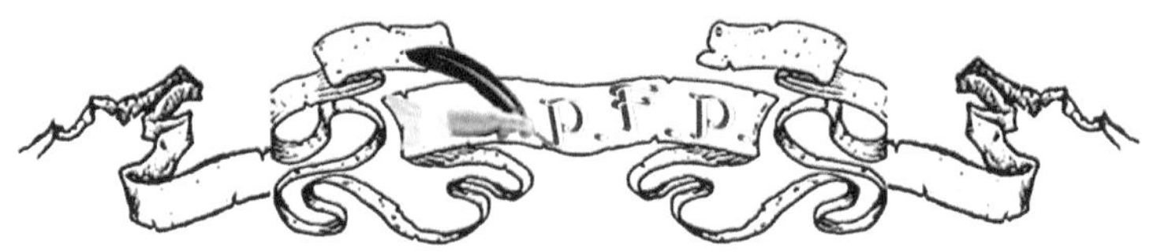

Count the Words

Empty days lonely nights

Count the words for moments bright

Remember to send a blessing can't think trite

© Dena M. Ferrari

****

Empty Days

Empty days, lonely nights
Are a terrible lonely trap
Don’t allow it for a moment
Give your face a slap

© Patricia Ann Farnsworth-Simpson

****

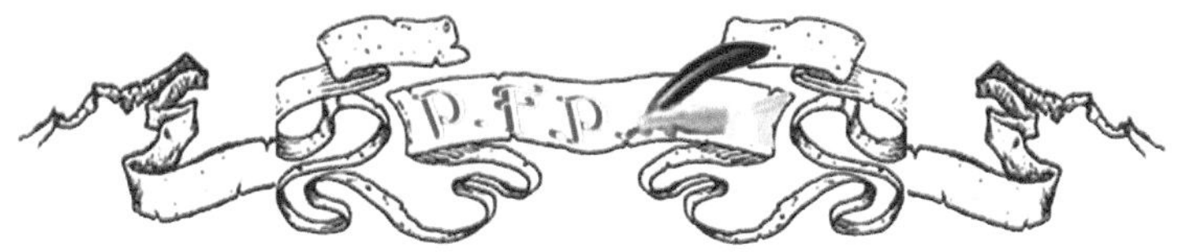

Robert Hewett Sr.

The Writers & Poetry Alliance

Poet Cottonwood

Robert Hewett Sr.
aka "Bob"

The Writers And Poetry Alliance
Laureate

http://www.apfpublisher.com/Cotton.html

****

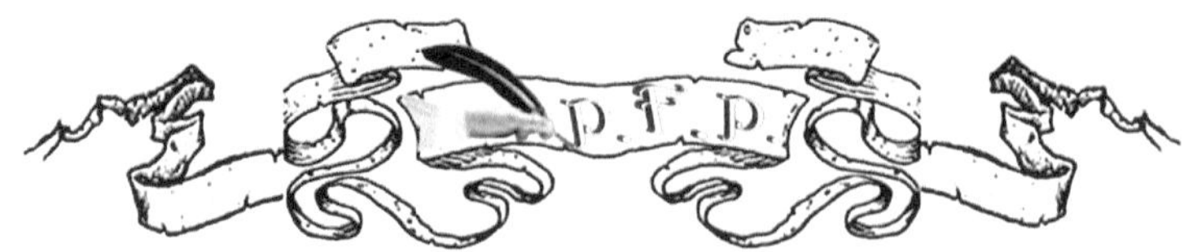

The Desert and The Forest of Life

(Starter Poem 18)

In the forest the wind blows free,
Whistling lightly swaying the tree.
Bird in treetop sings loud and strong,
Calling lover hurry along.
Great life in the forest each day,
Life in the Forest, a good way.

A small child lies listless and still,
Flies crawling, see no tears to fill.
His sunken eyes do seem to talk,
Why me, momma, why can't I walk?
No milk in his momma's flat breast
No food for her or for the rest.

Deer forage peacefully for food
God's creatures are in a fine mood.
Baby birds open their small beaks
Parents drop food to calm their squeaks.
The fawn and doe are links to life,
Nourished and playful, no strife.

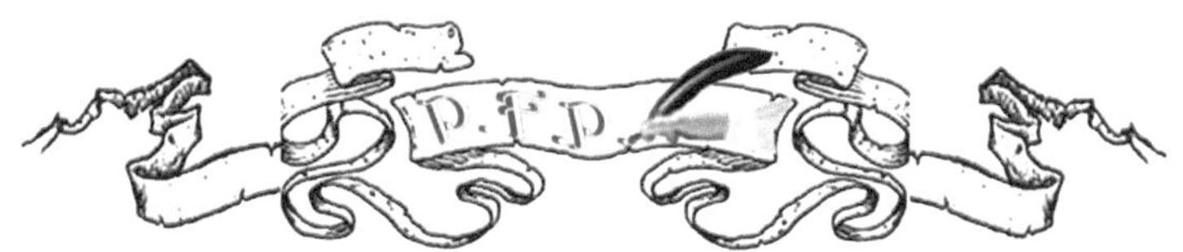

Somewhere in most any known town,
No money, or food to be found.
Baby's medicine can't be bought.
A child needs shoes just a lost thought.
People avoid them on the street
Somehow they don't deserve to meet.

Nature displays what God provides,
The forest gives its young delight..
God gave what man needs to be whole,
Man destroys, leaving only cold.
The weakest are starved with passion,
Claiming God's revenge, no compassion.

****

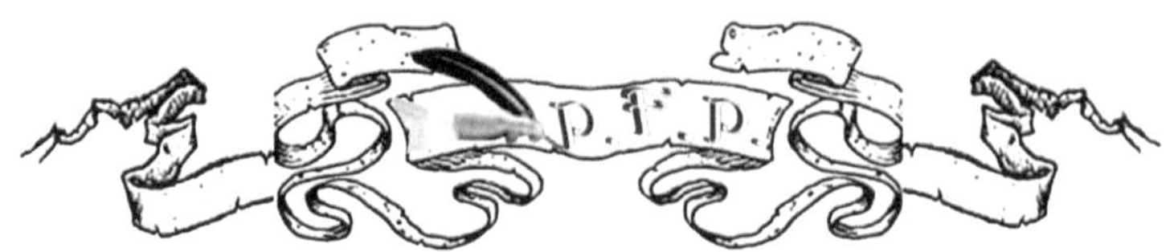

The Forest of Life

Whistling winds blow
Treetop bird sings
God's creatures forage
Small child listless
No food, milk
No baby's medicine
Weakest starved

© Christina R Jussaume

****

Hopeless

I walk
Lost
No food or rest.
People
I avoid them.
Listless.
No life
Just strife
On the street.

© Sue White

****

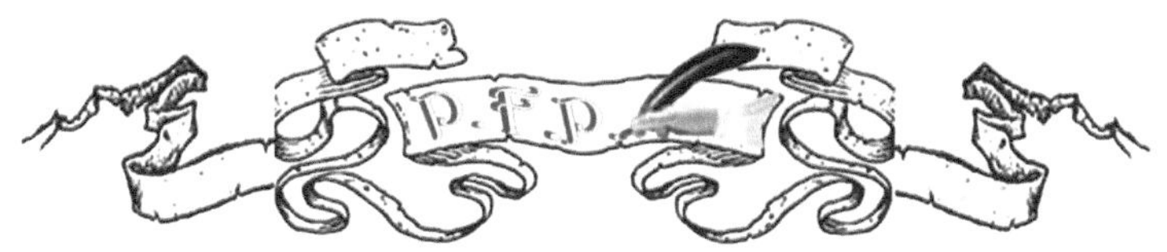

Desperation

People crawling on the street.

No medicine, food,

Creatures, forest.

Man destroys nature

The links to life

That God provides.

© Sue White

****

The Starved are Nourished

With nature man found life
Creatures in the forest
displays strong links
for the needs and
the starved are nourished

© Dena M. Ferrari

****

haiku

with forest whistling

small creatures calling hurry

playful squeaks nourished

Janet L. Vick

****

The Deer and A Bird

So peacefully the Deer forage

In the forest for food

A bird whistling in treetop

Loud in a playful mood

****

Patricia Ann Farnsworth-Simpson

AKA
Pat Simpson

www.patthepoet.com

****

Our Pit Week Holiday

(Starter Poem 19)

Hoorah! Were off on a holiday
The Pits shut down and we're on our way,
To the Miners Camp at 'Skeggy' we go
With family, friends and neighbours also!
To spend a week at the Miners Camp
Having fun competitions to see whose champ
Between our Pit 'Pleasley' that wants to beat
The other Pit 'Langwith' in every heat!
Competing is the fun, which we most enjoy
With encouragement given to each girl and boy,
In the races to be entered by everyone
From little toddlers to Dad and Mom,
There's the Egg and Spoon and Sack Bag race
And for those who keep a steady pace
The Marathon. Long Jump and Tug of War.
Where teams pull on a rope till one falls on't floor!
There are races in the pool and out on the sand
To see who can build the best by hand,
Mermaids. Sand pies and Sand castles too,
It's marvellous to see what folk can do!
The children have a party with games to play
And they're kept entertained all of the day,
There's Glamorous Grandma and Beauty Queen
A Fancy Dress and a Knobbly Knees!

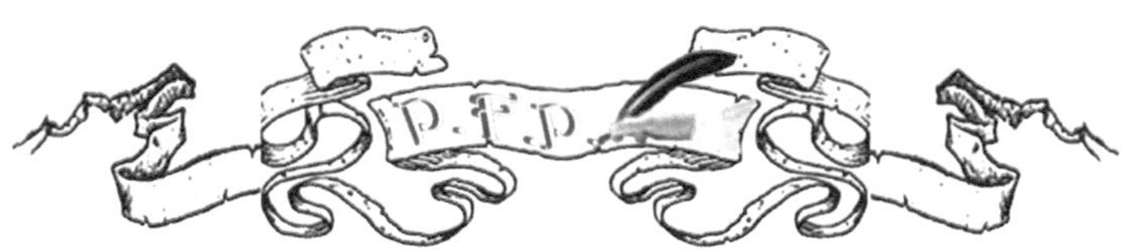

A talent competition where you can sing and dance
Tom bola or Bingo to take a chance,
Chalets to accommodate Parents and older kids
While little ones are put up in Dormitories
Where they all sleep together at the end of the day,
When the lights went out and they were tired of play!
But with sharing a room with twenty odd others,
Didn't lead to them being quiet under the covers!

For with half the kids coming from the other Pit
This made Pillow Fighting such a big hit,
But then when the fighting came to an end
Every kid in the dormitory was still a friend!

Then together they'd fall asleep, tucked up tight,
Leaving Parents free to go enjoy their night!
Out at the Pub, at a dance or a show
Having a good time with the friends they know!

Then at the end of the week with holiday done
And all the races have been run
Then it doesn't really matter which Pit won
As it was joining in that gave most fun!
Then they'd toast all the winners with a pint of beer
Promising to meet again to do same next year!
When both Pleasley and Langwith Pits will be
Having a Pit week holiday simultaneously!

Then with final "Cheerio" they shake hands with others
Coming from the other Pit that are now like Brothers,
And all the folk would be saying as they rode home on bus
Those folk from that Village are just same as us!
For like us on Monday the men too will go
Back down the Pit so far below!
Mam's will see Kids get back to school
And normality again will be the rule!

****

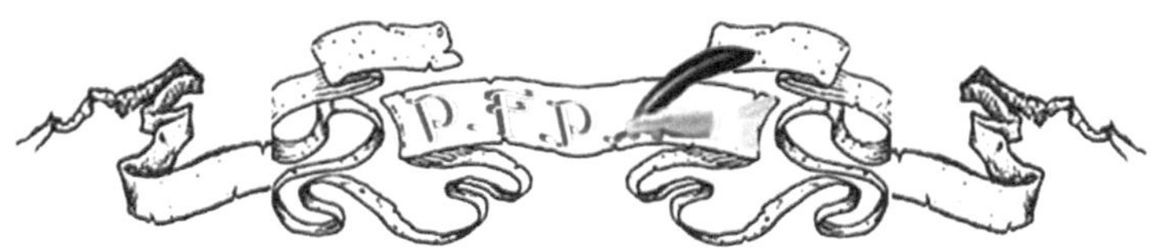

Hoorah

Pillow fighting gave most fun
In dormitories when day is done
Till asleep tired from play
Then parents toast "Hoorah"

© Patricia Ann Farnsworth-Simpson

****

Miner's Camp Holiday

Fun competitions
Each encouragement
The Marathon
Long Jump
Dance talent
Pillow fighting
Pleasley, Lanwith
Pit Holiday
Shake hands
Toast winners

© Christina R Jussaume

****

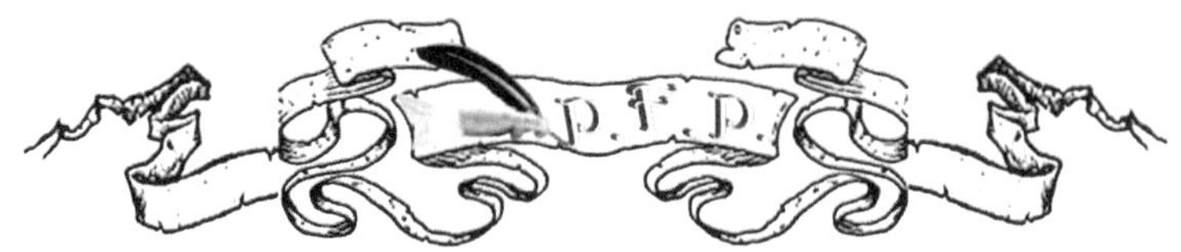

Together

Children together and having fun
sing and dance, play games with
family and friends, enjoy the night
They fall asleep

© Erich J. Goller

****

Grandma Can Dance

Grandma can dance
Competing against
the champ

In a dress all fancy
With marvelous encouragement
from Dad and Mom

© Dena M. Ferrari

****

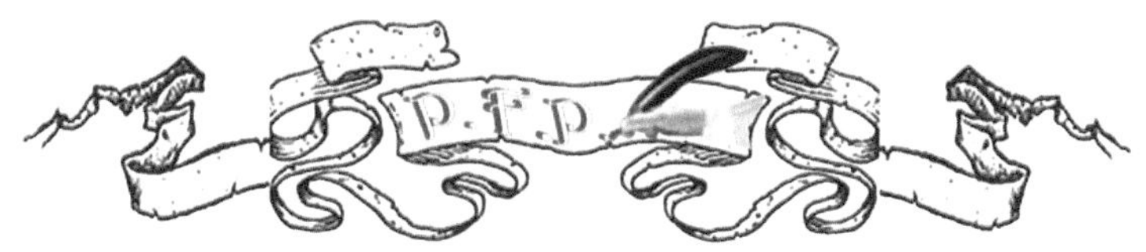

Hooray

The marathon champ
Races to beat
Everyone

Dad entered
the race
to have fun

Children encouraged
the winners
Hooray!

© Dena M. Ferrari

****

Mermaids

Mermaids out on the sand
Marvelous castles beauty show
Races from an older land
Dance in the village far below

© John W. Henson

****

Entertainment for Mermaids

The pit folk's children
Kept the Little mermaids entertained
With their party games
Leaving for home
Normality was back again

© George L. Ellison

****

Twenty Mermaids

Twenty mermaids
On holiday
Spend fun
At Castle Sand
Glamorous queen entered
To accommodate all
And entertained
By the pool

© Dena M. Ferrari

****

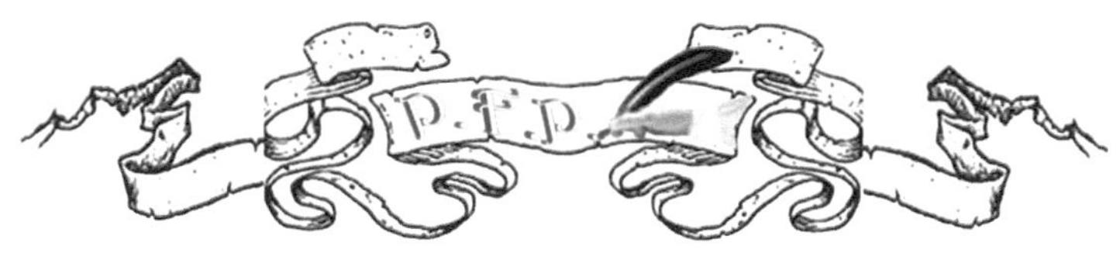

Senryu

competitions build

family encouragement

together in fun

© Janet L. Vick

****

Parents Have Fun

Kids in dormitories parents go
Out for night to play bingo
To take a chance
Sing and dance
Having fun

© Patricia Ann Farnsworth-Simpson

****

Time' is Nothing At All

(Starter Poem 20)

It’s tragic when children are waiting to see
Their mother gone to Heaven so they can be
Together again with God up above
In that angelic home so full of love

It must be hard when mothers look down and see
Their loved ones pining intensely
But then being there from hearing the call
They know that 'Time' is nothing at all

That it’s just an earthly man made thing
Without any value for Spirits that sing
For in Heaven 'Time' is always now
And in dreams Spirit can show us how

For in a dream together no matter what is done
It’s as if they’re still here and never been gone
For it's then one’s Soul comes to the fore
To let us join with others as before

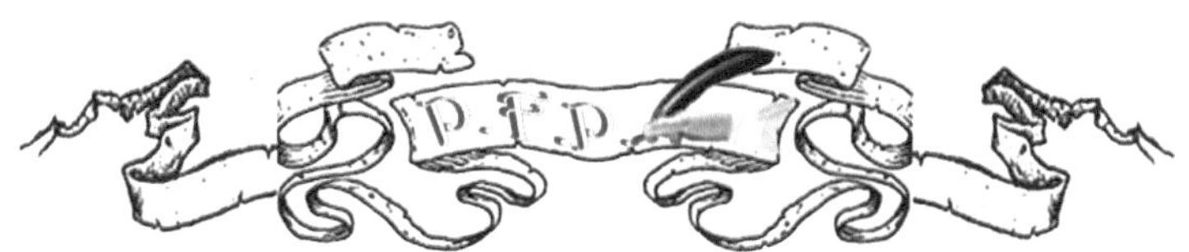

Yes! In a dream together if you laugh and play

That's how you'll be on the day

When you go join them then 'time' you will see

Is no longer in force to separate thee

****

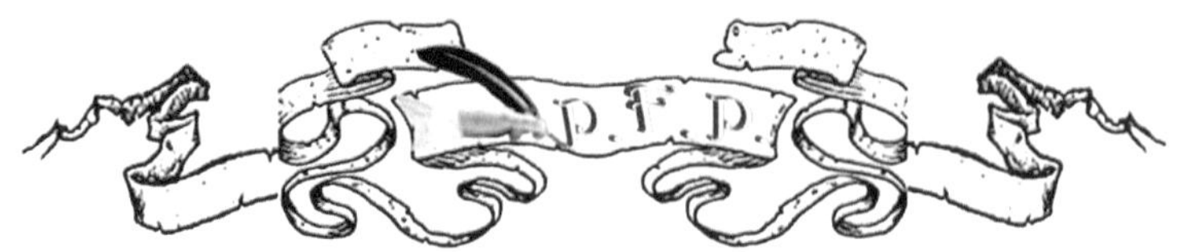

Mother's Dream

Mothers dream, children play
Intensely full of love
Their Spirits sing to God above
For the earthly time and day

© Patricia Ann Farnsworth-Simpson

****

Spirit Dreams

The earthly thing
for spirit dreams
and for ones soul is
to be always together
above in heaven
with God.

© Erich J. Goller

****

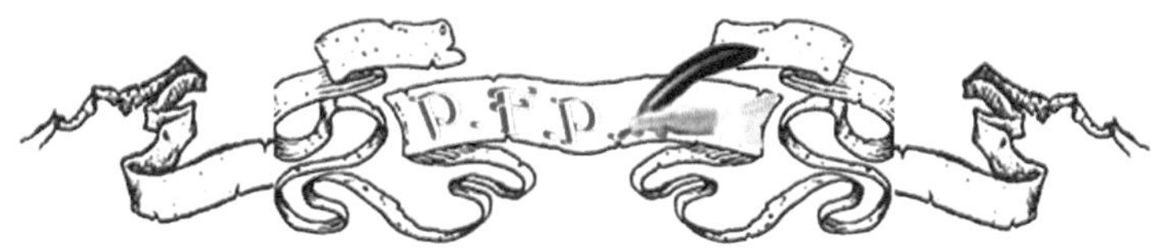

Together

time

to sing…

angelic

children show us

love

© Karen O'Leary

****

Time is Nothing

Children know that now is all

That time is nothing

Spirits can show us

To see and be

© Peter Duggan

****

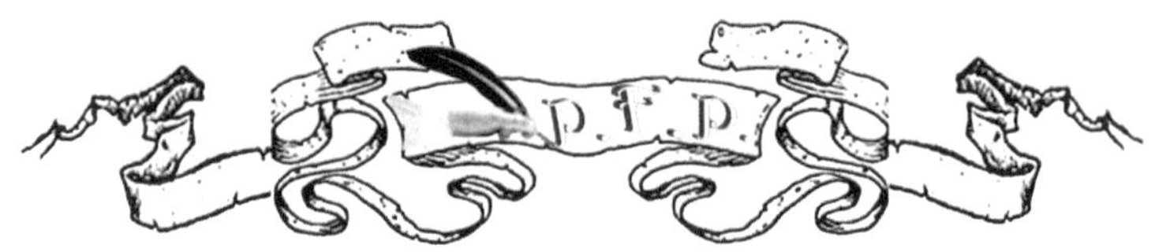

Angelic Home

Angelic spirits waiting
to see God up above
hearing the call in dreams
time will join all before
together again

© Rhoda Galgiani

****

Waiting Love

Waiting love...
Children pining,
never time,
no together.
Spirits dream
angelic call,
one's heaven comes before God.

© Janet L. Vick

****

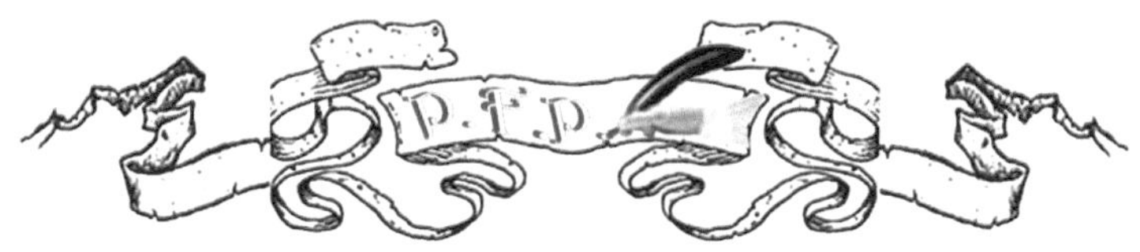

Angelic Force

Time Spirits
are hearing the children
laugh
Mothers see
them play
Together their value
is a force
that is angelic

© Dena M. Ferrari

****

The Soul of Time

The Soul of Time
is nothing without
love
The Spirits of Dreams
will sing to the children
intensely

© Dena M. Ferrari

****

Time

Heaven

Soul

Spirit

Value God

Above man

Again to be together

In time.

© Sue White

****

Intensely Full of Love

Spirits sing in Heaven

When you go up above

To join loved ones waiting

So intensely full of love

© Patricia Ann Farnsworth-Simpson

****

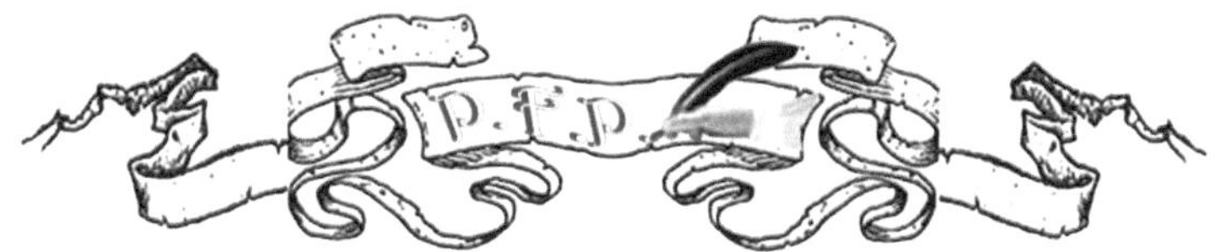

Our First Six Books

http://www.lulu.com/spotlight/patthepublisher

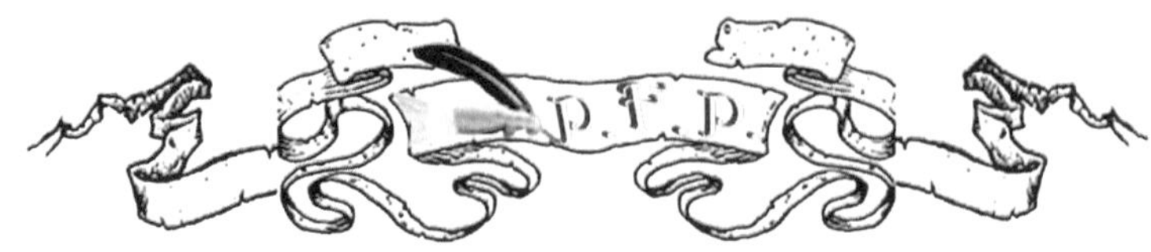

Alliance Poetry Styles Books

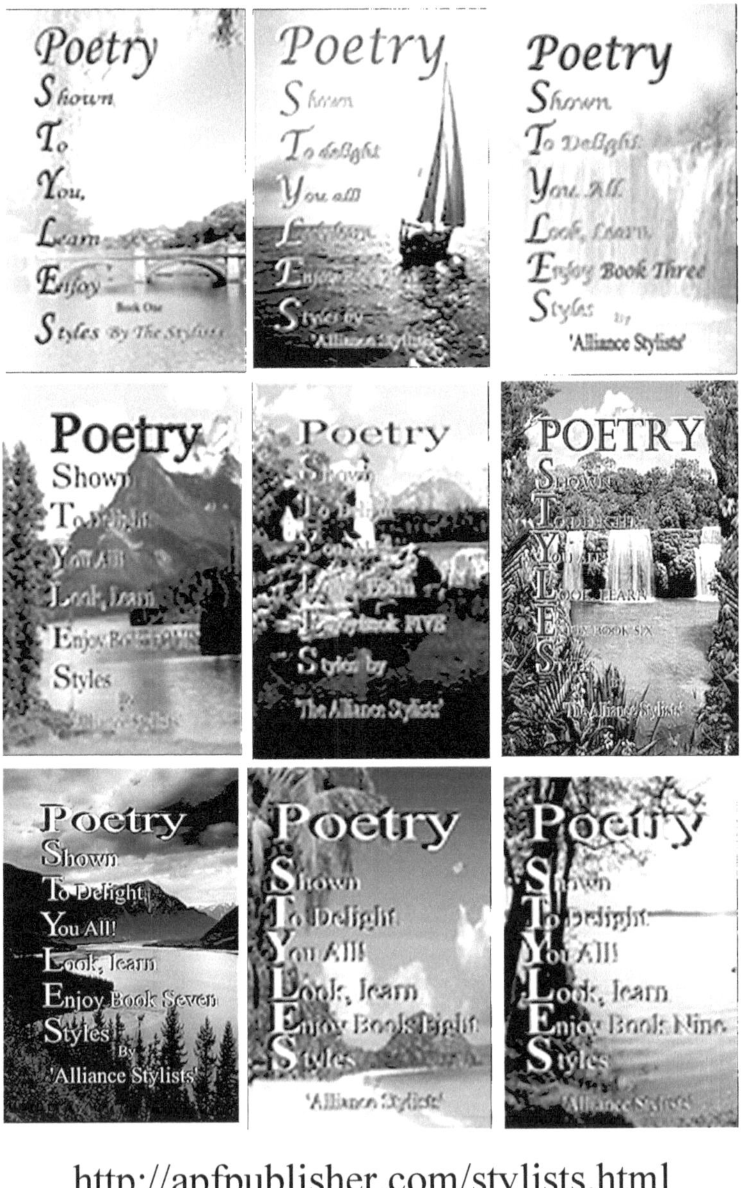

http://apfpublisher.com/stylists.html

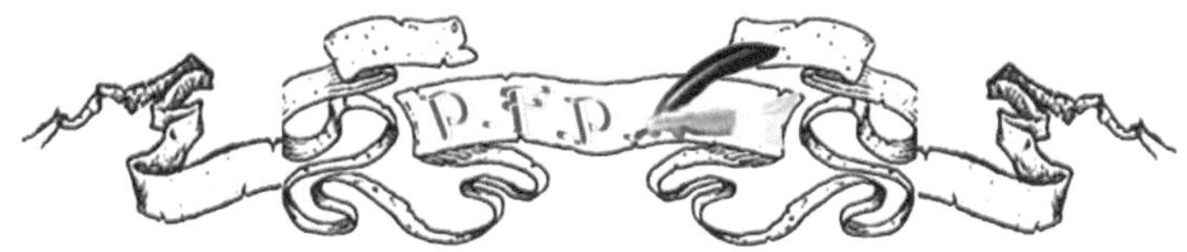

Some Fund Raising Books

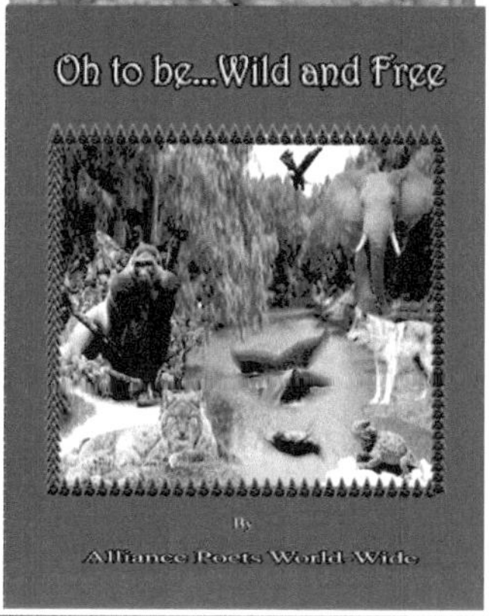

'Passionate Patriotic Poems'
9/11
Poets World-Wide

9/11 Ten Years On...
'Remembered'
In Words By
Poets World-Wide

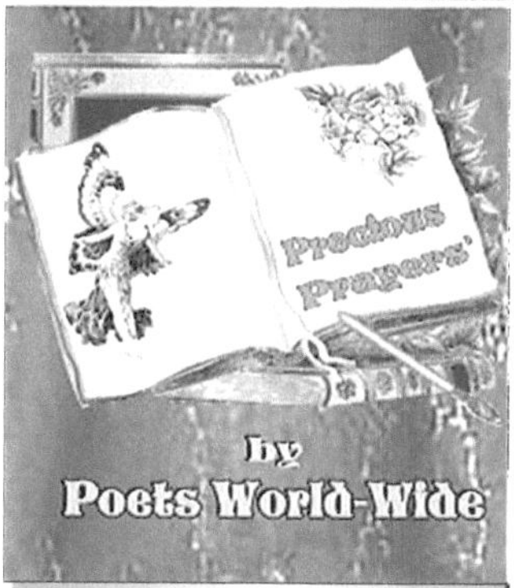

'Precious Prayers'
by
Poets World-Wide

'Poetic Words'
To Support the Troops
Poet's World-Wide

Cause for Paws
By
Alliance Poets World-Wide

Oh to be...Wild and Free
By
Alliance Poets World-Wide

---

http://apfpublisher.com/funds.html

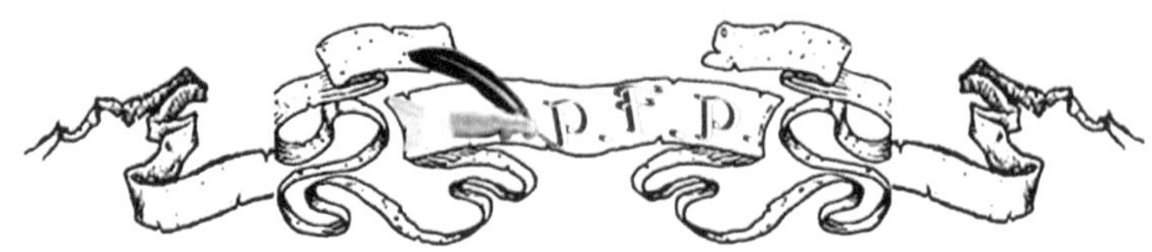

A.P.F.P.'S Authors & Books

Patricia Ann Farnsworth-Simpson Windows of Light,
Life's Carousel,Riding Life's Carousel: The Twinkles,
A Bundle of Muse, Flick The Karate Pig, Jack the Lad,
The Wizard, the Witch and Joe the Toe, Styles A-Plenty,
A Compilation of Tales to Thrill and Chill,
Stories to Thrill and Delight: Embracing Poetry with Style,

Carolyn Sconzo My Garden is Growing

Christina R. Jussaume: Amazing Pets and Animals:
Spiritual Living Waters: Joseph's Star of Eternal Promise:
To God Give the Glory: Spiritual Enlightenment:
Spiritual Encouragement: Spiritual Victory:
The Glory Unfolds Refresh Your Soul:

Dee Dawn Timeless Romance

Dena M. Ferrari Poetry From The Hearth:
Come Closer My Dearies:

Erich J. Goller -The Trojan Horse, Groovy,
My Candle Kept On Burning, For All Our Tomorrows,
Just For The PUN of It: Life's Magic Lantern:
Happiness Lives:Haiku, Senryu, Tanka: Love Yourself

George L. Ellison Poetic Reminisces: Weaving Words

Jacquelyn Sturge Live, Love, Laugh A Lot,
Live, Love, Laugh With Me Through Poetry A to Z

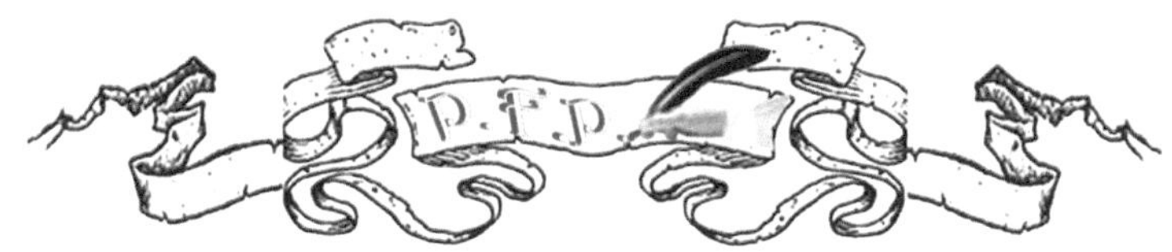

A.P.F.P.'S Authors & Books

J. Elwood Davis The Blue Collar Scholar

Jennifer Lee Wilson Fantasy and Foibles

Joanne Agee **Born** To Be A Rebel

Joe Hartman Pieces of Existence

John Henson

Shadow Dancer, Broken Wings: Darklingmire

Joree Williams Ariella - Living With Cancer

Joy Davis Cause for Paws

Karen O'Leary Whispers:Snippets an Anthology of Short Verse:

Katherine Stella Time For Haiku.

Kathleen Zvetkoff Embroidered Limericks

Kevin Bates The Gifts of Life

Lou Lenhart Life is a Gift Everlasting to Treasure

MAFLongfellow American Pie Poetry

Mary Ann Duhart From Out of The Pit I Cried, Duhart Expressions

Writing With Styles,

A Spiritual Breakthrough with Poetry

Michael L. Schuh But It's Mine, The Fruit of My Pen:

Mike and Joe, The Cross, The Porter Family

Spiritual Thoughts on Love and Life:

Mike's Choice Song Lyrics:

The Shiners Fix Up & Drink Up:

A.P.F.P.'S Authors & Books

Peter Dome Life, Love and Inspiration

Peter Duggan Simple Verse From a Simple Soul

Words from Heart and Soul:

Poets World-Wide For the Love of Japan, Alliance Stylists Series

Remembrance 1914-2014: The 'Magic' of "Michael Jackson"

Words of Love and Hope to Aid The Philippines

Quarter Moon Poet. Sojourners

Ralph Stott Legends for Lunch Time

Rhoda Galgiani Expressions. No Snow for Johnny:

Richard W. Lamp Ramblings of a Recovering Mind

Richard A. Rousay Choose The Right and Walk With Noah,

Choose The Right and Walk With Ruth, Walk With Alma

Robert Hewett Sr. Down The Road We Came: Thunderfoot

Roger L. Scott Letters from the Hills, The Last Trail Ride,

The Gifts of Pendrall

Rochelle E. Fischer Mystery In The Mist

Rosewood,: Poems & Promises

*All Authors can be seen on their own web page Here at www.apfpublisher.com

:

The Writers & Poetry Alliance

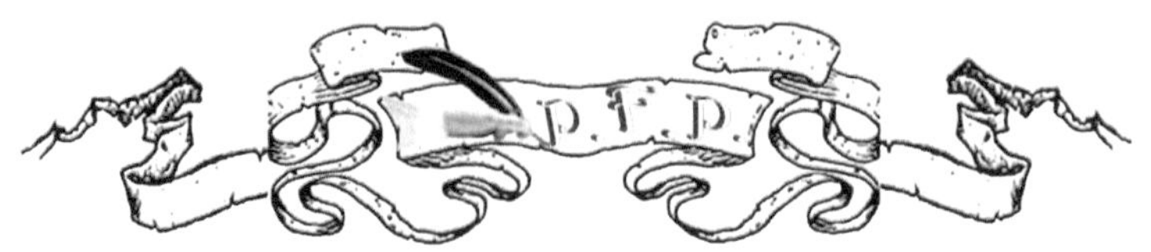

If You're A Writer
You'll Love The
'Alliance'

Poetry
Limericks
Stories

www.poetryandpublishing.com

"The Cyber Home For All Who Love To Put Pen To Paper"(To express thoughts, dreams and every inspiration)

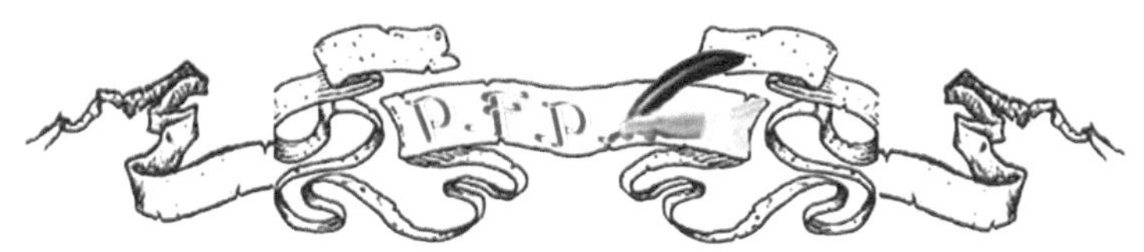
P.F.P.

A Passionately Fair Publisher
Always Here To Help You Achieve Your Literary Dreams
The Writers And Poetry Alliance
Bard
Fiction
Novels
Stories
Pat Simpson
Poetry
Rhymes
Fables
Contact E Mail: apfpublisher@gmail.com

****

www.ingramcontent.com/pod-product-compliance
Ingram Content Group UK Ltd.
Pitfield, Milton Keynes, MK11 3LW, UK
UKHW041943190726
13854UKWH00004B/1772

9 781329 403802